My Name Is 201

DALE O. GARRETT

D.O.G. PUBLISHING

Copyright © 2023 Dale O. Garrett & D.O.G. Publishing

FIRST EDITION

All rights reserved. No portion of this book may be reproduced in any form without the express consent of the author or his designee. Written and created, by a proud American. Printed in the United States of America.

DEDICATION

To Lynn, my rock, my love, and the most important person in my life, this book is dedicated to you. 'My Name is 201' is a title that represents my journey, my experiences, and my growth, and you have been with me almost every step of the way. Your unwavering love and support have been the foundation of everything I have achieved.

From my magic career to my law enforcement profession, our joint business venture as firearm instructors, and now my endeavor as an author, you have always been by my side. And even in more recent times as I developed medical issues, you have been there for me as my caretaker, showing me what true love and devotion looks like.

Words cannot express my gratefulness to you for all that you have done for me, and for being the person who brings so much light into my life. I know I could not have done it without you. My love for you is undying, and I hope this book serves as a testament to that.

Thank you for being by my side, for your constant encouragement, and for making every day of my life since the day I met you a beautiful one.
With all my love,
Dale O. Garrett

CONTENTS

1	What Do You Want To Be	11
2	Decision Time	17
3	I Didn't Sign Up For This	21
4	Single And Ready To Mingle	33
5	It's All Part Of The Game Brother	37
6	Brahma Drama & Bar Fights	45
7	The Bullet, The Prank, & The New Dispatchers	53
8	Which Forms Do I Use When I Shoot A Man	63
9	A Long Response Time & A Romantic Horse Ride	67
10	A Whole New World	73
11	A Peanut & A Shotgun	79
12	Operation Purity	85
13	More Monkey Business	91
14	The Magic Is Back	95
15	The Phoenix Rises	101
16	Frequent Flyers	105
17	A One-Man SWAT Team & The Appliance Store Burglar	113
18	Hitching A Ride	117
19	Police Pranks	123
20	The Prankster Gets Pranked	139

21	Adventures With Rick	143
22	Family War Stories	149
23	DARE To Be Different	159
24	My Eyes Are Watering	169
25	The Ugliness I Can't Unsee	173
26	What Is That Smell	179
27	The Beginning Of The End	183
28	The End But The Beginning	189

ACKNOWLEDGMENTS

I would like to express my heartfelt thanks to the following people:

Firstly, I want to express my gratitude to God for guiding me throughout the writing process of this book. Without His divine inspiration, I could not have completed this work. I am grateful for His constant presence and for the blessings that he has bestowed upon me. I want to also thank him for the opportunity to share this story with others. I pray that this book may bring laughter, insight, and inspiration to those who read it.

I am also grateful to Renee Eacret and Fred Moorse, for their invaluable feedback and for helping me shape the manuscript into the best version of itself.

Thanks also to all of the people who are mentioned in this book and to those who aren't who have been a part of my life story. I offer my sincerest gratitude. I am a rich man to have you all as friends.

Last but in no way least, I want to thank my wife Lynn, who provided unwavering support and encouragement throughout the writing process. Without her love and patience, this book would not have been possible.

INTRODUCTION

Greetings & thank you for purchasing this book! I'm the author of "My Name is 201." 201 was my first ever call number that I was assigned when I officially became a law enforcement officer. I'm excited to tell you my story - a story of living two lives with equal passion and success.

As a police officer and a professional comedy magician, I've experienced many personal challenges & adventures, & I can't wait to share them with you. Every story in this book you are about to read is 100% true. I did however change the names slightly because it would have been too monumental of a task to get signed releases from everyone I mention.

This book takes you on a journey through my eyes, as I balance the dangerous job of being a law enforcement officer with entertaining audiences & making people laugh. You're going to get a kick out of reading about some of the hilarious & elaborate practical jokes I pulled on my fellow officers too!

I'm not just telling you my story in this book; I'm celebrating the human spirit. Throughout my life, I've faced many obstacles and tragedies, but I like to think that my unwavering determination, resilience, and faith in God have always helped me overcome them. I have always firmly believed that humor was just as crucial to me as performing my important duties as a police officer. It provided me a necessary balance.

As you delve into my story, my antics, practical jokes, & pranks, which brought laughter and happiness to those around me, I hope you'll be reminded of the significance of humor in your own daily life.

I wrote this book because I wanted to share my story with others & inspire them to never give up on their ambitions. I'm honored to have had the privilege to live out my dreams and laugh all along the way.

So, turn the page and join me on this fun, inspiring, & unforgettable journey.
Dale O. Garrett

Chapter 1 - WHAT DO YOU WANT TO BE?

The Boy Magician

Ask any young boy what they want to be when they grow up and you're likely to get a variety of unique answers.

However, there are a few answers that seem to pop to the top of the list more frequently than others. Oh, sure there's the outlandish, silly careers kids come up with such as pirate or robot. But the most frequent answers are policeman, fireman, or a football/basketball player.

I personally would always respond to that question with one of two different answers, a police officer or a professional magician. My aunts in Maryville, Tennessee after hearing one of those responses would pat seven-year-old me on the head while throwing their own heads back in laughter. I wondered why they laughed at my responses.

Did they not think it was possible? Perhaps it was just difficult for them to imagine little me as a grown, rough and tough police officer and maybe they thought the idea of being a magician was just as outlandish and silly as wanting to be a pirate or a robot.

At seven years old, there wasn't much I could do to prepare for a career as a police officer other than playing cops and robbers with my cousins or other neighborhood kids. There was always one condition when I played that game though. I HAD to be in the police officer role, never the robber.

Now, doors to my other career path of being a magician seemed a lot more open to me. I received magic sets at Christmas time and for my birthdays. I consumed every bit of knowledge I could get my hands on from the magic books in my school library.

Anytime a teacher would assign us to do a book report, I without fail, would choose a biography on Harry Houdini. I remember we would have to stand in front of the class and tell everyone what our book was about. I had read so much about Houdini that I could recite his exploits from memory.

While most of the kids were shy and stumbled their way through their book reports, I spoke with authority and passion on my book. My poor classmates got an education about the history of magic and the Great Houdini during every oral book report we were assigned – whether they wanted to hear about the topic or not.

At first, I performed my magic tricks mainly for my mother and father and friends at school. Eventually I put together a little show and created hand-made flyers on notebook paper which I passed out door to door to all the houses in my neighborhood. The crudely made flyers promoted my magic show on Saturdays with an admission price of only ten cents!

As my magic show began to take shape and improve, my mother, who for some reason fully supported my ambitions to become a professional magician, began to book shows for me. She never learned to drive, but would spend hours on the phone calling civic clubs and organizations and cajoling them into hiring her son – the boy magician – to perform for their group. Her efforts were quite successful! My father would then chauffeur me to my "gigs."

As a finish carpenter, my father also built a lot of my magic props, special tables, and backdrops that I used in my shows. They were both so supportive of my then hobby and future career. I remember them both beaming with pride as they would watch me perform.

Since I was seven years old, I have performed so many magic shows there's no way I could even begin to guess the number of performances I have done over my lifetime. I continued to perform shows into my middle school and high school years but slowly, my attention was distracted from magic and I became more interested in girls. Yep, I was a typical thirteen-year-old boy.

My love of magic however, never went away. It would eventually make a huge come back in my life. I'll share the details of that resurgence a bit later in this book.

Policeman. A new beginning

About the time I turned fifteen, I heard about an organization run by our local law enforcement agency, The Lake Wales Police Department. It was called the "Police Explorers Post." Law Enforcement Explorers was a hands-on program which was open to young boys and girls who had completed the 6th grade.

The program still exists today. It was for young people interested in a career in law enforcement or a related field in the criminal justice system. The program promoted personal growth through character development, respect for the rule of law, good citizenship, and patriotism.

As a member of the Police Explorer Post, I would get some classroom training at our monthly meetings and be allowed to ride along with real, full time police officers in actual police cars! I would get to do some pistol shooting and learn gun safety. I would be able to participate in some community policing at local festivals and parades. I would get to experience firsthand what it's like to be a police officer!

I couldn't have had my mom sign me up for this fast enough! I thought to myself, even way back then, "this is the beginning of my law enforcement career!" And you know what? I was right! It wasn't long after I had become a Police Explorer however, that tragedy struck.

In the small town of Frostproof Florida, a town just south of Lake Wales, a police officer named David McCally responded to a silent alarm call at a bank. The bank's alarm had a recent history of malfunctioning.

Believing this was just another malfunction, Officer McCally pulled up to the front doors of the bank about the same time the bank robber was exiting. Officer McCally was shot in the head before he could even exit his patrol car and instantly died on the scene from his injury. He was killed just five days before his 22nd birthday, and less than three weeks after getting married.

Several days later was the funeral service for Officer McCally. Our group of Police Explorers from the Lake Wales P.D. was invited to attend. My Police Explorer buddy, Arnold Wootley and I were excited and honored to be a part of it. Arnold and I had started in the explorer program about the same time and had become fast friends.

So, about ten of us Explorers loaded up into a van driven by our Police Explorer advisor and headed south to the funeral. The closer we got, the more police vehicles I saw on the roadways.

At the huge church where the ceremony was held, there were hundreds and hundreds of police cars and police motorcycles from all over the state of Florida and even some from other areas of the nation. It was a sea of blue lights. I had never seen anything like it before in my life!

The church was packed! Every seat was occupied. The only place for us lowly Police Explorers to view the proceedings was to stand along the wall of the church.

We were fortunate though that even though we were forced to stand way over to one side by the wall, we were positioned relatively close to the front of the church.

Our Police Explorer advisor warned all of us to bend our knees slightly as we would be standing for quite a while. Bending our knees would keep us from passing out. It was hot inside the church. With so many people there, it was clear that the air conditioner was struggling to keep up.

It was a solemn affair. My heart ached for the young bride of the officer as she was helped to her seat on the front row, sobbing uncontrollably. I was sad for her, yet strangely fascinated with the protocol of a police funeral and was interested in seeing the rest of the ceremony. But that wasn't meant to be.

About two songs into the beginning of the service, just as that second song ended and the place was eerily silent, I for some reason, glanced over to my left. My buddy Arnold was two explorers down from where I was standing. I guess I was glancing over toward him to see his expression and gauge his reaction to the enormity of what we were witnessing.

Just as I looked over at him, what I saw seemed like it happened in slow motion. Arnold fell face forward like a tree that had just been chopped down at its base. He had done EXACTLY what we had been warned against doing. He had locked his knees and it cut off his blood flow causing him to pass out.

The sound he made when falling into the church pew in front of him sounded like a wheelbarrow full of potatoes being dumped out all at the same time off of a second story roof. The commotion caused everyone in the church to turn our direction to see what had happened. I was embarrassed for myself, for Arnold, and for all of my fellow explorers.

On his way down, Arnold's face bounced off the corner of the church pew in front of him causing a pretty significant gash just above his left eye. Our explorer advisor decided we should take him outside to get some air and attend to his bleeding wound.

So, all of the explorers were instructed to follow. Once outside, it was decided by our advisor that because of Arnold's injury, we should all leave the funeral service and return to Lake Wales.

I felt bad for Arnold, but I was a little miffed at him too for making us all miss this important event. Unfortunately, later in my police career, I would have the opportunity to attend a number of other officer's funerals who were killed in the line of duty.

Nobody was ever arrested for McCally's murder however, there was a primary suspect who was believed to have been the killer. That person died while in prison for other crimes.

I don't know why as a kid I wanted to see that first police officer funeral so badly. They are such sad, sorrowful affairs. As an adult, they make you ponder your own mortality and the fact that the person lying there in the coffin deceased, could have just as easily been you. It could have been you because you had responded to similar calls many times during the course of your career.

There but for the grace of God go I...

Chapter 2 - DECISION TIME!

So, I'm now fifteen years old and my best friend Charles came over to visit with some exciting news! "I got a job!" he exclaimed. "I start on Monday!" I said, "that's great man! Congratulations!" He went on to say that the fast-food restaurant where he had been hired (the one with the king, not the clown) were still hiring and I should apply for a job there too so we could work together.

I wasn't really interested, but my mother who was in ear-shot was! She agreed with Charles that I should get a job. After all, I had a mo-ped for transportation and the restaurant was only 5 minutes from my house. I reluctantly applied and was hired. Thus began my work life at a real job. Gone was my innocence of youth and the luxury of my parents paying my way in life.

I became a model employee. I was trained both in the kitchen to make sandwiches and the front-line taking orders and running the cash registers. My work-life was humming along well. But my personal life was ...complicated.

I started dating a girl from my high school named Susan. Susan was a troubled person. She came from an abusive family. Her mother drank a lot and I later came to learn that her father, an over-the-road truck driver, sexually abused her and her sister when he was in town.

I guess in a way, I felt sorry for her. Scratch that. I definitely felt sorry for her. I wanted to play the role of "the knight in shining armor" and take her away from that terrible environment she was living in. I wanted to save her. But I couldn't very well do that on a fast-food employee's salary.

We continued to see each other in high school until eventually she was removed from her home by Social Services and was placed with a foster family in Lakeland an hour away. We stopped communicating. She wasn't allowed to call me and I had no idea where she had been relocated to.

I went on with my life, but wondered what had become of her. I graduated high school and continued to focus on my career in fast-food. But I still had a burning desire to become a police officer.

I was now nineteen years old and it was decision time! Because of my dedication and excellent work ethic, I was recommended by my manager to go into management training. But first, I had to get past a big interview with the regional boss of the corporation. The interview was set for about a week away on a Monday.

But then, something miraculous happened! I had also during that same time period, applied for the position of deputy sheriff at the Polk County Sheriff's Office. I had taken a polygraph, passed a psych exam and drug test, and had a background check conducted on me. They called and wanted me to interview next week on Wednesday – only two days after my fast-food management interview. The Sheriff's Office interview was the final step in their screening process and from what I heard, was a formality if everything else had checked out – which it had.

I went to the fast-food management Interview on Monday and the big boss seemed very pleased with my qualifications and was happy with the recommendations from my supervisors who had seen management potential in me. He offered me the job on the spot!

My first instinct was to blurt out, "I'll take the job!" But instead, knowing the Sheriff's Office interview was coming up, I asked for a few days to think about it. He seemed a little surprised. I didn't tell him why I needed to think about it. This was probably not the response he expected but he agreed and told me to let him know my decision soon.

Fast forward two days later. I interviewed with the Sheriff's Office personnel manager. At the end of the interview, he shook my hand and said everything looked positive but he would let me know definitively within a few days. A few days later I got a call from him to let me know that the job was mine!

I had two job offers in front of me. A fast-food manager or my dream job as a law enforcement officer. It was an easy decision for me but I did find it a bit awkward having to go back to the big boss at the corporation and say thank you, but no thank you.

As I was finishing out my two weeks' notice at the restaurant, I was working the closing shift. They had a crew called "porters" that would come in after we closed to clean the grease hoods and do more specialized cleaning than what the employees could do.

The crew that took care of our restaurant and several others in the county was cleaning after we had closed and I mentioned to one of them named Daryl that he won't see me around much longer because I was going to become a deputy sheriff. He was not a pro-law enforcement type person. In fact, he seemed like a druggie burn-out type. He made fun of me, oinked at me like a pig every night during those two final weeks, and was generally very condescending toward me.

Several years later, around three o'clock in the morning, I was running radar on Havendale Blvd. in Winter Haven. A car doing sixty-eight miles per hour in a forty-five mile per hour zone, zoomed past me. Once I got the car pulled over, guess who was in the driver's seat? My old buddy Daryl.

He was between cleaning the chain's restaurants and was running late to get to the next one located in the city of Auburndale cleaned before the restaurant's morning crew arrived to open for the day. I made him even later and wrote him one of the most satisfying traffic tickets of my law enforcement career. I made sure he remembered who I was before I released him to go on his way. I'm sure he hated cops even more after that incident, but hey, if you don't want speeding tickets, don't speed! Oink, oink!

Chapter 3 - I DIDN'T SIGN UP FOR THIS!

At some point during the hiring process at the sheriff's office, someone broke the following news to me. Because I was only nineteen years old, the powers that be decided that I should mature a bit before they put me out on patrol to protect and serve.

I was given the choice to spend a year working in the jail as a corrections officer or a year in communications. I didn't like it. I wanted to be out in the field on my own. But hey, if this was the path I had to take to get there, then so be it. I didn't complain or protest.

I had heard through the grapevine that if you begin working in the jail, it was really difficult to get transferred out to work the road. So, I opted for communications. I should note that due to a shortage of sworn officers, my year in communications was shortened to only seven months.

This was a GREAT choice and I'm happy I made it! I met some wonderful dispatchers like Vickie, Perky, Gail, Susan (not my future ex-wife, a different Susan), Calvin, Rita, and Donald to name a few - some of whom are still my friends today. I learned a lot working with them. It gave me a lot of respect for the people behind the radio.

It taught me to not be high-strung and scream into the microphone when requesting back-up and tensions were high. If the dispatcher can't understand what you're saying, they don't know where to send you help. During my time in communications, I heard a number of deputies do this and I learned from their bad examples not to duplicate their mistake when I got out on the road myself.

As a teenaged Police Explorer at the Lake Wales Police Department, I was introduced to the concept of law enforcement officers having their own unique language for communication. However, during my time in communications at the Sheriff's Office, I came to fully understand and appreciate the importance of this specialized language for effective communication among my fellow law enforcement officers.

This language is known as "cop speak" and it is designed to be precise and concise. One example of cop speak is the use of terms like "white male" or "black male" to describe a person. While some people may find these terms impersonal or perhaps offensive, it's important to note that as police officers, we are trained to use this type of language as part of the job. By using precise and objective language, we could communicate important information quickly and effectively, which can be critical in emergency situations.

In addition to using descriptive terms for people, deputies and police officers also use 10 codes and signals to describe certain crimes and situations. These codes and signals are a shorthand way of communicating important information quickly and efficiently. For example, a police officer may use the code "10-18" to indicate that they are responding to an emergency call using their lights and sirens. Or they may use "Signal 10" to indicate a stolen vehicle. While in communications I took the initiative and instead of relying on a printed card with ten codes and signals like some deputies did, I committed them to memory. Not just the frequently used ten codes and signals, but every single one of them.

Something else I learned from working in communications was not to sound grumpy on the radio or be lazy and try to pass calls off to other officers. Even if it was out of my zone or assigned area. If they dispatched me to it, I took the call without arguing or complaining.

Later in my career, at different times, I had Kaye, Jennifer, Sherri, and Juanita - dispatchers at the Winter Haven Police Department – compliment me by saying how cheerful or upbeat I always sounded on the radio or how calm my voice was during pursuits. My cheerfulness on the radio was very intentional. I like to think that it helped in a small way to brighten the dispatcher's day and make his or her shift just a tiny bit more enjoyable.

Dispatchers have a difficult job. Working the radio and taking phone complaints myself really opened my eyes to the stressors of that part of the job. It gave me a greater respect for them when I did finally get transferred to the road. It made me a better deputy.

FTO training

With my time in communications cut from one year down to only seven months, I was sworn in as a full-time deputy sheriff at the age of twenty!

You know, it's funny. I was now a sworn deputy sheriff and carried a gun eight hours per day on duty, but if I needed some ammunition to go to the gun range for practice, I had to take my mom to the gun store first to buy it for me. It was a little embarrassing. The legal age to purchase ammo was and still is twenty-one and there were no exceptions for law enforcement officers.

My dream had come true! But I wasn't ready to be Polk County's newest crime fighter just yet. First, I had to complete my Field Training Officer (FTO) education. Typically, the field training process lasts about six weeks. You spend those six-weeks riding with an experienced deputy who has been through specialized classes on training and evaluating rookie deputies.

I was assigned to the Winter Haven area. It was an area of the county that I was completely unfamiliar with. My FTO was named Dave Dunnawate. He was an older guy, well, older than twenty-year-old me anyway. He was probably in his forties. He was a good guy, but the entire training period that I was with him, his mind was on other things.

He was in the process of going through a bitter divorce and would come to work sad, depressed, or sometimes angry. To his credit, he never took his emotions out on me, but there were many nights where the conversation silence was just – well, awkward.

One night, he directed me to drive to a neighborhood and park in front of a house. He said, "wait here. I won't be very long." I had no idea whose house it was or what was going on, but it soon became clear to me. I heard him arguing with a woman – his estranged wife.

The argument was fairly loud and became pretty heated. I wasn't sure what to do. I thought about going up to the door to ask if everything was alright, but I was just a probationary trainee. I didn't want to get in the middle of their argument, make him mad at me, or risk him washing me out of the program.

On the other hand, I was bearing witness, at least auditorily, to what amounted to a domestic dispute. Just as I was about to open the patrol car door and go in, he came out of the house in a huff, slamming the front door behind him. I didn't know exactly what they were arguing about and I had enough sense to not ask. I figured if he wanted me to know he would tell me. He didn't.

More silent patrolling for the rest of that night.

Outside of his marital issues, Dave was a great FTO. He taught me one of the most valuable lessons in law enforcement that I ever learned. One that has stuck with me my whole life. The lesson was "Know where you are at all times."

On this particular evening, Dave was in a good mood. He was driving the patrol car and I was riding shotgun. Suddenly, he pulled over and said, "BANG! I've been shot! Where are we at?" I quickly looked around for a street sign but he had intentionally pulled over in the middle of a block where there were no street signs visible. Dejected, I bowed my head and replied, "I have no idea." He explained how important it was to know what street you are on and the nearest cross-street at all times. That way if something happened, and I needed help, I'd be able to tell dispatch where to send the calvary.

A few hours later, we had finished our lunch break and began patrolling again and chit-chatting. Once again, he unexpectedly pulled over in the middle of an unfamiliar area to me and said again, "BANG! I've been shot! Where are we at?" He had gotten me again! I had no clue and admitted to him that I had no idea where we were. He gleefully said, "Gotcha again! Two to nuthin'"

At that point, I realized that this was not only sort of a little game we were playing, but also a teaching method he was using. I told him, "You got me a second time, but I can guarantee you, there won't be a third."

Later on, when he thought I wasn't paying attention, he quickly stopped the car again and repeated his now familiar phrase, "BANG! I've been shot! Where are we at?" I quickly responded, "we're on Old Dixie Highway just east of Delon Court!" "You win that round," he said as he grinned a big grin. He knew that his unique, subtle way of mentoring me was starting to work. I was paying closer attention to my surroundings.

He tried the same little "game" a lot more times but I won every time. After that second time he got me, I was determined to NOT let him get me a third time! Every intersection we went through, I was looking out of the corner of my eye at the street signs. Eventually, after learning the street names, I didn't have to watch them as closely unless we were in an area I hadn't been before.

Due to the department being shorthanded on deputies county-wide and the fact that Dave saw me as a quick study, instead of six weeks of FTO training with Dave, I only spent seven days with him. I was issued my own patrol car and was assigned to the Lake Wales area – my hometown and the area where I grew up.

I used his technique of always knowing where you are when I started patrolling on my own and later when I went to work for the Winter Haven Police Department. It was so helpful in learning the streets.

I even used it when I myself became FTO certified to teach the auxiliary officers and young Police Explorers who would sometimes ride with me. I still use it now that I'm retired even though now, I could easily rely on my GPS to tell me where I am. Old habits die hard.

An unfortunate reconnection

A couple months before transferring out of communications to work the road, a new county Sheriff was elected. His name was Dan Dumasse. (That's not his real name, but it fits him so I'm using it. I'll explain why later in the book).

About the same time the new Sheriff was elected, I reconnected with Susan. She was still living with the foster family and wanted to see me again. We made a lunch date and I picked her up. She told me that her biological father had gotten her pregnant which is why she was removed from that environment by Child Protective Services. While at the foster home, the baby produced from that rape died of sudden infant death syndrome. She was devastated. She also dropped another bombshell on me.

She claimed her foster father had also been molesting her! She had turned eighteen and my desire to save her by playing "knight in shining armor" kicked in again. I told her that now that I'm making more money, we should get married and get her out of that situation. She agreed and within a week, we said our "I do's" at the county courthouse in Bartow. The plan was for her to move in with me at my parent's house until we could get an apartment of our own. And that's what we did.

My mother didn't like Susan from the get-go. She had a mother's intuition about her. She thought Susan was trouble. I never told my mom about all the personal struggles and trauma that Susan had suffered out of respect for Susan's privacy. In fact, I've never disclosed them to anyone until now.

As the days went by, I seemed to always be trying to smooth ruffled feathers of both Susan and my mom when they would argue about little things.

One day, my mom pulled me aside and told me that she had some checks missing from her checkbook and suggested that Susan was the culprit. No checks had been written on her account and when I approached Susan with the allegations, she categorically denied knowing anything about it. I believed her. Tensions continued to build between the two of them, and I decided it was time for us to get our own apartment.

My own father was battling lung cancer at this time and I just wrote the whole missing check thing off to my mother being distraught and a bit scattered and forgetful. Shortly after we moved into the apartment, my father passed away in August. It was emotionally devastating to me to lose my father, but I somehow managed to push forward.

So, there I was. Married at a young age, my mother at odds with my new wife, and my father dead. I didn't sign up for any of this…

Mother is always right.

In our apartment and married just short of two years. Life seemed to now be moving along in a more positive direction. I was finally a full-fledged deputy out on patrol on my own. I had a take home patrol car. They assigned me my own call-number. It was #201 (which I always pronounced "two-oh-one" when I used the radio).

That number was special to me because it was my very first call number. It represented my personal achievements. It represented all of my hard work, staying out of trouble as a kid, staying away from drugs as a teen, keeping a clean record as a young adult, and completing the police academy to reach my goal of becoming a law enforcement officer.

Susan had gotten a job as a cashier at a grocery store in Lake Wales. With our combined two incomes, we were definitely not rich, but we were getting by comfortably.

Then, one day just after I had finished my day shift and got home and changed out of my uniform, I got a call from Charlie Fontane. Charlie was one of the detectives who worked out of the same sub-station that I worked out of. He wanted me to come down to the sub-station immediately, but he wouldn't tell me why. I thought it was some sort of prank, but the tone in his voice sounded very serious.

My curiosity piqued; I drove down to the office immediately. When I walked in, I said, "Hey Charlie, what's up?" He said, "c'mon back." I followed him to his office. He closed the door behind us. He sat down at his desk and turned on his tape recorder. Then, he read me my Miranda rights!

I was so confused and didn't understand what the Hell was going on. Then he dropped this bomb on me; "Your wife has been arrested." "WHAT!?" I exclaimed in disbelief. "Is this a joke?" He assured me it was not a joke and that he himself had booked her into the jail only a few hours ago.

He went on to explain to me that Susan had stolen some elderly woman's check book and had forged several checks to get money. I was shocked at what I was hearing. I was gob smacked! Then he asked me about our financial situation and whether or not we were struggling. I said, "No, not at all. Between her paychecks from the grocery store and mine from the sheriff's office we're doing ok."

Then he flat out asked me if I had any knowledge about her taking the woman's checkbook or obtaining money by forging her checks. "Absolutely not! I am completely taken off guard by all of this!" I replied.

My mood began to shift from one of shock to one of anger. Not at Charlie mind you, but toward Susan. Charlie was a good detective and a trusted friend. I didn't doubt his investigative skills in the least. Not for even a second! If he said she had done it, I believed him. I just didn't understand WHY she had done it.

I'm sure Charlie could sense from my words and emotions that not only did I genuinely not know anything about the stolen checks and forgeries, I was beyond furious at Susan for doing this. For stealing from an old person. For putting my dream career in jeopardy. For embarrassing me in front of my colleagues.

Charlie ended his interview with me and clicked off his tape recorder. He told me that Susan would probably be released from the jail with a court date in the next hour or two if I wanted to go to Bartow to the jail to pick her up. Oh, I was going to pick her up alright! I had a ton of interrogation questions for her myself!

As I drove to the jail, my head reeling and still seething about this whole mess, the memory of my mom missing those checks from her checkbook popped into my head. I knew without a doubt in that instant that my mother had been right about her all along. "She most assuredly had stolen my mom's checks" I thought to myself.

I picked Susan up at the jail. I was humiliated even walking in there. Word had spread quickly that Susan was a deputy's wife. I felt everyone there was side-eyeing me and judging me as I was standing in the lobby waiting for them to bring her down from lock-up.

We began the long drive back to our apartment. I'm not going to lie, there was a LOT of yelling on my part during that drive and when we got home too. She never was able to give me a reason why she did what she did. I'm not sure she even knew why herself. But I did know this; she had irrevocably shattered my trust.

She admitted to me during our heated discussions over the next week or so even more shocking news! She admitted that she was regularly smoking pot - a habit that she had successfully hid from me. She also admitted to me that she had slept on several occasions with a co-worker – a bag-boy at the grocery store where she worked. She said she would do this while I thought she was working late, or while I was on duty. She said she never brought the guy to our apartment and that they always went to his place where he lived with two roommates to have their trysts.

Who knows if that was true or not? I couldn't believe anything she said anymore.

No matter what was in her past, her behavior now was reprehensible and inexcusable. I had offered her a new life, a positive path forward. A way to make her future brighter and better than it had ever been up to the point we were married. She threw it all away. She destroyed my trust in her and my faith in our marriage. It was over.

A very few short weeks later. We were divorced in Bartow at the same courthouse where we had been married. I never spoke to her again after that.

Chapter 4 - SINGLE AND READY TO MINGLE

I willingly gave Susan everything in the divorce. The furniture we bought, the television, towels, dishes. Everything. I wanted no reminders of that dark chapter of my life. Starting back at square one from scratch, I moved back in with my mom. Since she didn't drive, she needed the companionship and rides to the store and doctor appointments anyway since dad had passed away. It was convenient for both of us. Other than the many "I told you so" comments about Susan, she welcomed me back with open arms.

A while later, without any real bills to speak of, I bought myself a motorcycle and later, a Fiero. I loved that little car. I loved its sleek lines, the stereo speakers built into the headrests, and those oh-so-cool pop-up headlights. It was as close as I was ever going to get to owning an Italian sportscar. Plus, it had a lot of cool-factor when I would pick up girls for dates.

I say "dates" like I was some sort of playboy. Truth is, I only went out with four or five girls until I found my real true love. Much more on her a little later. I was living large! As I'm putting all this down in words for this book, I realize that I definitely had a "type" in mind when asking girls out. It wasn't as much about their hair color or looks. It was more about what line of work they were in. I gravitated to girls who were "on the right side of the law." I dated two dispatchers, a female police officer, and a clerk who worked in Bartow at the courthouse. What were their common denominators? They all worked at jobs related to the law. They all had background checks conducted on them to work where they worked. I was gun-shy about associating myself with any criminals ever again. Even being that selective, I still had a real problem trusting anyone. I never wanted to repeat an experience like I had with Susan!

Are you a cop?

One day, I hopped on the motorcycle and went over to my childhood friend Charles' house to hang out. He wasn't home so I began driving back toward my mom's house.

It was a beautiful day. The sun radiated brilliantly, casting a warm and inviting glow that illuminated everything in its path. The sky was a pristine blue, devoid of any clouds, creating an unbroken expanse of azure overhead. The temperature was ideal, though it may have been a tad on the warmer side for those unaccustomed to Florida's climate. The air was heavy with humidity, hinting at a possible late afternoon thunderstorm, yet it was still pleasant enough to be outside and soak up more of that sunshine. I was thinking to myself, "do I want to go back to my mom's house or should I just take a scenic drive to nowhere in particular?"

About the time I had that thought, a lady in a car, driving the opposite direction, turned across my lane of traffic into her driveway. I wasn't speeding, but I wasn't going slow either. There was no time to stop. My motorcycle T-boned her car and sent me flying over my handlebars, over the hood of her car, and if memory serves, I also cleared a row of mailboxes on the other side of her car before hitting the ground.

That's as far as my memory of the accident goes. Although I was wearing my helmet at the time, the impact knocked me out cold. I'm sure the poor lady must have thought she had killed me. I wasn't moving or responding. Someone frantically called an ambulance and my next memory was slowly coming to and feeling the paramedic pressing up and down my arms and legs checking for broken bones.

When one of the paramedics got down to my ankle, I heard him say something about "an open fracture." An open fracture is when the bone breaks and then pierces the skin. He pulled up my pants leg to get a better look. The bulge that he thought was a protruding bone was instead the butt of my .38 caliber snub nosed revolver that I was carrying in an ankle holster.

A bit more coherent now, I became more aware of what was going on when the paramedic who had found my gun began asking me, "Are you a cop!? Are you a cop!?" He seemed very concerned about what I did for a career. I managed a mumbled response, "yeah, I'm, I'm a deputy sheriff." The look of relief on their faces that I was a good guy and not a bad guy was very noticeable.

They wanted to take me to the hospital to be checked out, but after just a few minutes I was feeling fine and had hopped up to my feet as if nothing had ever happened to me. I felt 100% fine. Ah, to be young and resilient.

I gave them and the driver of the car my name and information for insurance purposes. The Highway patrol had been called but it would be hours before they could respond. They were spread pretty thin back then. I walked on back to my mom's house which was only about a mile or so away.

Later that evening, I took a shower and noticed that my entire groin and upper left leg were severely bruised and had turned a lovely shade of purple. To be perfectly honest, it kind of scared me at first. It looked really bad.

I had apparently scraped my "no-no area" and upper thigh across the fairing of my sport bike as I was catapulted across it. My groin was slightly sore, but I told nobody about it. Especially my mom - because she would have wanted to see and assess the injury, and I was much too old for my mother to be seeing my winky-dinky.

The State Trooper finally came by the house and talked to me about the accident. He gave me a case number and said that he had talked to the other driver already and the stories matched up and that he would be citing the other driver for failure to yield right of way. The bruising finally went away and I was back down to just the Fiero and the patrol car for transportation. The bike was totaled.

Chapter 5 – IT'S ALL PART OF THE GAME BROTHER

I first met the guy I'm about to describe to you around 1984. Cocaine was king of the street drugs at the time, especially a newer derivative called "crack" or "rock" cocaine!

It offered the user a faster more intense high and had become quite prevalent on the streets. It was also more addictive. "Rock Monsters," as we called them, would do just about anything for their next hit of it - to include burglary, theft, robbery, prostitution, and even murder.

I was a 20-year-old rookie deputy sheriff and got word one day during our briefing from my sergeant that I was being pulled from patrol and temporarily assigned to the Sheriff's under-cover narcotics unit. I didn't know why they selected me at the time, but in retrospect, I assume it was because I looked so young and the drug dealers would be less likely to suspect I was a cop. I was told to report to Detective David Walton.

I knew of Detective Walton, or "Wally" as most people called him. He had a reputation as an amazing narcotics detective, but I had never met him before. He was considered a "rock-star" among undercover drug investigators within the county! I mentioned that most people called him "Wally" but I never did for some reason. To me, he was always "David."

I pondered that first morning on what to wear. I went with black slacks, a white dress shirt, and a sportscoat to conceal my shoulder holster. I debated on whether to wear a tie, but decided to just roll it up and stick it in my jacket pocket and go with the open collar look. If I needed the tie later, I would have it with me. This clothing choice would later prove to be an unfortunate decision.

When I first met David Walton, he looked pretty much like a long-haired hippy. I thought to myself, "is this guy really a cop? He looks like a ne'er-do-well with his long hair and his shabby clothing." Of course, that was all just a façade. I always thought he looked a little like the famous magician, Doug Henning, although I never mentioned that to him. No reason really. He would have probably gotten a good laugh at the comparison.

From the front, the narcotics division office looked like any old boring, nondescript business in an industrial park with no foot traffic whatsoever. There was a fake business name on the door, but I won't mention it here, or the city it was in, just in case they're still using it today. It was very "secret squirrel" type stuff!

You entered through a small, bland, ordinary looking 10' X 10' lobby. There was no indication on the walls of the lobby of what this "business" really was. A secretary in the lobby had to buzz you into the main part of the building. Past that second door, there was a beehive of activity. The office was laid out like any white-collar type office. Imagine an office with a lot of cubicles, but no cubicle walls. It was an open floor plan and you could survey the whole room from pretty much any location.

There were lots of detectives who looked like they themselves should be in prison for something. Some looked like they were rounded up and brought there by bus straight from the biker bars in Daytona. Others looked like they were transported there by a time machine from Woodstock. Some looked like wannabe lead singers from a 1970's rock band. One looked straight up like a homeless wino. They were all working at their desks and walking about. It was like a setting I had only seen before in movies!

As I followed behind David enroute to his desk, he stopped briefly in the hall to have a conversation with his supervisor about a case that he had been working on. I could feel the glances from the other detectives in the room.

I don't know if they didn't trust me or if they were just curious about the newbie entering their secretive office. I didn't look anything like them. I was clean shaven, had a close-cropped haircut, and was wearing a damn sportscoat! UGH! Why did I wear a sportscoat!? I felt like I stuck out like a turd in a punch-bowl. I looked less like an under-cover narcotics detective and more like an assistant youth pastor at a non-denominational church!

Despite my dimwitted choices in clothing, David seemed to take a shine to me right away. He was super friendly and so very nice to me. I could tell right away that he was a "people person." He asked me if I had ever bought dope before. I replied, "of course not." He slightly grinned and asked, "not even a joint?" Again, I replied in the negative. Slightly surprised, he asked, "well, you've at least smoked pot before, right?" Again, I responded in the negative.

I explained to him that I had always been some-what of a straight arrow and that I had wanted to be a cop from a very young age and never would have dreamed of doing ANYTHING that might jeopardize my career path – to include smoking pot. Plus, it would have really disappointed my parents. Every bit of that was the God's honest truth. He sighed and said, "OK, first thing's first, you need to look a little more civilian and a lot less cop when you come in tomorrow." I felt like taking off that damn sportscoat and hiding underneath it!

The next day I returned to the secret narcotics office wearing jeans to conceal my ankle holster, an old rock radio station t-shirt, and the oldest pair of sneakers I owned. I tried hard to emulate the "look" I had seen the day before on all the other detectives. In retrospect, I probably still looked like Beaver Cleaver, but in a faded radio station t-shirt...

When I arrived at David's desk, he surveyed my clothing choices and said, "that'll work! But you need a few more things." He rummaged around in his desk drawers and produced a short haired brown wig, and a worn, greasy looking ball cap and said, "here put these on, because we're throwing you into the deep end today. You're going to make some drug buys."

I have to admit that my heart raced a bit at the prospect of buying illegal drugs and this whole new "dark under-world" that I had been catapulted into at the tender age of twenty. Other than my first day and a brief chat with David about how to act like a druggie in the car on our way to the area where we would be doing the first drug buy - that was all the training I had to be an under-cover narcotics detective. Even though David had sort of taken me under his wing, I felt woefully unprepared for this!

The plan was simple enough though. I was to drive up in a car to these known street level dealers, ask for twenty dollars in rock cocaine and after making the transaction, return to where David and another detective were waiting and watching with high-powered binoculars (This is way before the development and wide-spread use of micro cameras). I would give them the dope for testing and logging into evidence and we would all later do affidavits on the perps and pick them up on the felony warrants issued at a later date.

The first two buys went surprisingly smooth! Very quick transactions! Way faster than any fast-food purchase that I had ever made! I was beginning to gain some confidence. Then, we changed locations again.

At the third location there was no good place for David and the other detective to park and surveil the buy from. So, they parked in a nearby strip-mall around the corner to wait for me.

I pulled up as before and the dealer approached my driver's side window and asked, "what'chu need, what'chu need!?" I replied. "Rock. Twenty bucks." Suddenly, he reached in and grabbed the money with his left hand. I grabbed his arm and a violent struggle ensued!

He was tugging and pulling and I was determined to not let him go. Then, to break my grip on his arm, he punched me square in the left jaw with his other fist! It stunned me briefly and I released my grip. He ran away with my buy money! I wasn't sure what to do! I asked myself, "Do I get out and chase him or what!?" After thinking about it for a few seconds, I decided to maintain my cover and just drove off.

I returned to where David and the other detective were waiting and told them what had happened. I thought they would be upset with me for losing department money and not bringing back any product. But they weren't. They made sure I was OK, and then sort of chuckled and joked around about me getting robbed.

I apologized for losing the department's money. David smiled that broad smile he was known for and said, "That's all part of the game brother!" I thought to myself while rubbing my sore jaw, "I don't think I like this game very much."

The rest of my time in narcotics was spent mainly doing clerical stuff, a couple more uneventful drug buys, and participating in a few warrant arrest round-ups and drug raids. It seemed surreal wearing a ski-mask as a law enforcement officer. But hey, I guess some good-guys wear masks. Think Bruce Wayne's alter ego.

I believe toward the end of my two-week assignment, everyone, including myself, mutually decided that I wasn't under-cover narcotics detective material and I happily went back to the patrol division. Besides, it was only supposed to be a temporary assignment anyway.

U/C work takes a special breed of law enforcement officer. Some are better at it than others. It wasn't my cup of tea. I later found that my talents were better utilized on the prevention side of the drug problem when I became a DARE officer at the Winter Haven Police Department. More on that experience later in this book.

David, over the years, went on to climb the ranks within the Sheriff's Office and eventually went to work at the Florida Department of Law Enforcement (FDLE) working major drug trafficking cases - both domestic and international. He became a pretty high ranking muckity-muck at that agency too, bringing down major players from foreign drug cartels.

He was REAL GOOD at what he did! Because of his sole efforts, untold amounts of drugs were taken off the streets. Many, many dangerous drug dealers and manufacturers were put out of business and into a prison where they belonged, and countless lives were surely saved.

Once he retired, he volunteered tirelessly as the coordinator for the Marine Corps Toys For Tots of Polk County to make sure the economically challenged children of our community received Christmas gifts every year. In fact, he was the driving force behind that organization for a lot of years - and was recognized nationally for his efforts! David was one amazing guy and I was proud to call him my friend!

As he aged, his hair, mustache, and goatee became snow white and he incorporated that look for several years at Halloween time - dressing up like Colonel Sanders. What a great sense of humor! Ask anyone who knew David and they'll tell you that like me, he reveled in making people laugh.

After retirement, my wife Lynn and I would occasionally see him out at restaurants and he would always make it a point to come over to our table to chat and say hi or snap a selfie picture with us.

The last time I spoke to him was back in August of 2022 when one of my other books had launched. He called me to offer words of encouragement, congratulations, and was absolutely thrilled and excited about the project.

Not too long after that, David suddenly fell ill with an aggressive brain cancer, was hospitalized, and passed away only weeks later. My heart ached for his family and his hundreds, maybe thousands of law enforcement friends and fans from here in Florida and around the world.

I'll miss my one and only "drug buy buddy." Rest in peace David. I don't know why God called you home so soon. I guess it's all part of the game brother.

Chapter 6 - BRAHMA DRAMA AND BAR FIGHTS

It's the big one Elizabeth!

I think one of the many things that attracted me to a career in law enforcement was the variety of the job. When you put on that uniform and strap on that gun belt to begin your shift, you never knew what the day or night was going to have in store for you.

I was assigned to the East side of the county. It's commonly referred to as "The Lake Wales Ridge" or shortened by the locals to just, "The Ridge." The ridge refers to an actual sand ridge running for about 150 miles south to north in Central Florida. Clearly visible from satellite, the white sands of the ridge are located in Highlands County and Polk County, and also extend north into Osceola, Orange, and Lake Counties. It is named for the city of Lake Wales, roughly at the midpoint of the ridge.

Lake Wales is my hometown and I was assigned to work out of the Lake Wales Sheriff's Office sub-station. Eastern Polk County has a LOT of rural areas. There are areas that you can drive for miles and miles and see nothing but pine trees and cow pastures.

One especially foggy night, around three o'clock in the morning, I was called on the radio by dispatch. "Bartow to 201." "Two-Oh-One go ahead." "Be enroute to Highway 60 near the area of River

Ranch Resort in reference to assisting on a signal four. FHP has been notified and is also enroute." River Ranch is the only thing on highway 60 for many miles around. It's situated in one of those very rural areas I mentioned. It's sort of a western dude ranch type resort. A signal four was a motor vehicle accident and my role was to stand by and assist in any way I could until the Florida Highway Patrol arrived. The trooper was quite far away and would be delayed in getting there.

I couldn't get there too quickly myself. As I mentioned, the fog was really thick that night. When I finally did arrive, I saw a horrific scene! A single vehicle, a large white Cadillac convertible was still partially in the road with its flashers on and steam slowly rising from the demolished engine area and into the cool night air.

The front end was smashed all to Hell and there was blood EVERYWHERE! More blood than I had ever seen before! It was on the front of the car, on the smashed windshield, the white leather interior. Everything was covered in blood.

The driver of the car, an older black gentleman was sitting well off the roadway in the grass. He was wearing a white suit and he too was covered in blood. But here's the weird part. There wasn't a second vehicle around anywhere. I rushed over to the man to check on his wellbeing. It was then I was hit with an odor most foul. It seemed that in addition to the blood, the man was also partially covered in feces! After inquiring if he was injured, he replied "I'm fine. This ain't MY blood."

He wasn't injured at all but, as my mom used to say, "he was madder than an old wet hen." His voice and mannerisms reminded me of Fred Sanford from the 70's TV show that bore his name. He was very animated and comical as he waved his arms around and he told me the story. I had to stifle my laughter several times during his description of what had happened.

"What happened here!?" I inquired. "Well sir, I was coming down the road in my new car. Oh, she was a purdy one. Leather interior, cassette stereo, the works! I just bought the damn thing two months ago. Anyway, the top was down and I was enjoying the breeze and the night air listening to my jazz music cassette. And then I hit an invisible wall! Next thing I know, my car's all busted up and I'm covered in crap and blood!"

I said, "invisible wall? What are you talking about man?" He said, "you know when you've got your headlights on and it's foggy out, and everything in front of you looks white?" "Yeah," I responded. "You know what else is white? Damn Brahma bulls!" And then, he gestured toward the grass area about 15 feet off the roadway and slightly behind where his car was.

I shined my flashlight into the darkness in the direction he pointed and there it was. A 1,200-pound dead Brahma bull that had exploded on impact, rolled up the windshield and had apparently been catapulted into the darkness. I hadn't even seen it up until that point. The hapless bull had wandered out of its nearby pasture and decided to park itself in the eastbound lane of traffic, perfectly camouflaged by the thick fog.

When the trooper arrived on scene, he was initially equally as horrified. And then, like me, was also amused at the animated driver and his humorous description about what happened.

Excuse me deputy. Excuse me.

Working the Ridge area of the county back then, one thing was certain. We were spread pretty thin. Usually there were only three of us covering that entire 25% of the county.

On this particular Saturday night, there was only two of us. My only co-worker was tied up working a death investigation when I got dispatched to a domestic disturbance at The Laflama Bar.

They sent another deputy to back me up, but he was coming from Bartow so I knew my back up was probably at least twenty minutes away.

The Laflama (Spanish for "The Flame") was a hole in the wall, dive bar. It catered almost exclusively to the large Hispanic population in the area. Being in the heart of Florida, citrus groves were plentiful. Every year the area was inundated by migrant workers, many of whom had come here illegally from Mexico to work the groves. Picking fruit is hard manual labor and these people on the weekend liked to let loose!

When I arrived, I was met in the parking lot by a Hispanic woman named Rosita. She had a contusion just above her left eye and it was pretty significantly swollen. She spoke to me in broken English and curse words enough for me to understand that her husband was the one who had hit her during an argument in the bar.

The domestic abuse laws in Florida were pretty straight forward. If one spouse claimed abuse and there were physical signs of injury, an officer of the law was mandated to take action and arrest the offender.

After she confirmed to me that he could understand English, I asked Rosita to come into the bar with me and point out her husband. As we entered the bar, she identified him as one of the individuals standing at the bar. He was wearing jeans, a white western style shirt and a white straw cowboy hat. After I confirmed with Rosita that he was her husband and was the one who had hit her, I approached him and asked him to step outside so that we could speak. The very loud Hispanic music made it almost impossible to hear a person talk to you even if they were standing right next to you.

He ignored me. I shouted again a little closer to him to step outside with me. The last thing I wanted to do was to have to arrest him inside the bar where some of his buddies might come to his aid and cause even more trouble. This time, there was no doubt in my mind that he heard me. Again, he ignored me. I put my hand on his elbow to indicate I wanted him to come outside with me. He jerked it away. Again, I put my hand on his arm and he made the worst mistake he could make for someone in that situation. He shoved me away from him.

The fight was on! Not only did I have him for domestic battery, but now he had committed battery on a law enforcement officer. We began struggling against the bar. I've got to admit that although I was young, strong, and agile, I hadn't been in very many fights. Like I said earlier in this book, I stayed out of trouble growing up. The thought crossed my mind that my back up was still probably by this time ten to fifteen minutes out. I was pretty much on my own.

The man was drunk, belligerent, and resisting me with everything he had. I finally managed to get him spun around and pinned his body between my own body and the bar. I reached back and removed my handcuffs from their holster on my duty belt and began struggling with him to get his arms behind his back. Success! Well, half-way success anyway. I got one arm behind his back and cinched down the cuff around his wrist. I was trying my best to grab his other arm which was flailing about as I was struggling with him when something odd happened.

In the middle of this wild bar fight with this angry drunken man, someone began tapping me on my back as if to get my attention. I ignored it because I was a little too busy at the moment to stop what I was doing and answer a question or give someone directions to a theme park. Still the tapping on the lower right side of my back continued. I finally got the guys left hand twisted up behind his back and was able to cinch down the second handcuff restraining him.

Still the tapping on my back was taking place. Now at a point in the fight where I could finally turn a bit to see who was tapping me on the back, I did so. Much to my surprise, it was Rosita! And she wasn't tapping me with her finger. She was stabbing me repeatedly with an ice pick she had picked up off of the bar!

Apparently, she had caller's remorse and decided that she A) didn't want her husband to go to jail, and B) took offense to us fighting with each other. In an effort to assist her husband, she was actively trying to kill me! That as you can understand, made me a bit angry. I let her husband go from my grasp and spun around to deal with her. Without any thought at all about her being a female, I punched her square in the face as hard as I could. She dropped the ice pick and fell backwards to the floor covering her now bleeding nose with her hands.

With an overabundance of adrenaline now coursing through my veins, I seemed to develop super human strength. I didn't have a second set of handcuffs on my duty belt so I grabbed the back of her shirt with one hand and her husband by the scruff of his neck with my other hand and escorted them both outside to my patrol car. EVERYONE in the bar had stopped what they were doing to take in the show. We didn't have cell phones back then but if we had, I bet that everyone would have been rolling video.

I got the husband in the back seat and retrieved my second set of cuffs from my car. Mrs. Rosita was cuffed and put in the back seat with her husband who she had, not more than forty-five minutes ago, called the Sheriff's Office on. I had no more than slammed the back door of my patrol car when my back up from Bartow came screeching into the parking lot. He smiled and said, "Looks like you've got everything under control." Still breathing heavy and trying to catch my breath, I told him, "This chick tried to stab me to death with an ice pick in the bar!" His expression changed to one of concern and asked, "are you ok?" "I think so" I replied.

"Watch these two for a minute, I've got to go back in there and get that ice pick for evidence." "No problem" he said.

I went back in and was quickly able to find the ice pick still on the floor near where Rosita fell down after she had sniffed my fist. I took it back outside and the other deputy asked, "where did you get stabbed?" I showed him and we pulled up my shirt and Kevlar vest so he could assess my injuries. There were surprisingly only a few small wounds to my back. The bullet proof vest had stopped most of her stabs with the ice pick from getting through. Kevlar vests aren't designed to stop something like that. I shrugged it off and took Mr. and Mrs. congeniality to the jail in Bartow and booked them in.

It was only later as I was examining the ice pick that I realized why the vest had stopped most of the penetrations. The tip of the ice pick was bent from being well-used in the bar. The curved tip was blunt enough to keep it from piercing through the vest and going into my kidney. I surmised that the shallow wounds I did receive were the times she had missed the vest slightly. If she hadn't been as drunk as she was and her blows had been a bit more forceful, there's no doubt that it would have caused me a lot of serious internal damage. I thank God that He was looking out for me that night.

When I got home later after work, I cleaned the wounds with peroxide and smeared some antibacterial ointment on them. Just like after the motorcycle accident, I didn't seek medical attention. Can you tell I'm not a fan of hospitals? In retrospect, I probably should have at least gotten a tetanus shot. There's no telling what kind of germs were on that rusty old, nasty ice pick.

Chapter 7 – THE BULLET, THE PRANK, AND THE NEW DISPATCHERS

My mom, the worrier

My mom was a worry wart. She always was for as long back as I can remember. Most of her worry was centered around her five sons and their safety. To her worrying equaled love. Perhaps she had good reason to worry since my brothers and I were always doing crazy, dangerous, or un-wise activities to occupy our time. Like the time as a kid when I jumped off our two-story roof with a parachute that I had fashioned out of a bed sheet. But I digress.

When I became a deputy sheriff, my mom was understandably, always worried about me. I always tried to down-play the danger and make her think my job consisted of assisting little old ladies in crossing the street and helping children find their lost dogs. But I'm sure she saw through me. She knew there was real danger associated with my career choice.

Once when I was in uniform and about to leave the house to begin my shift, instead of her standard, "be careful at work." she made this comment, "be careful tonight because there might be a bullet out there with your name on it."

The next day, I was cleaning out a junk drawer in my room when I came across some tiny self-adhesive letters. I had an idea! I spelled out "DALE" with those letters on the side of a brand new .38 caliber cartridge and showed it to her. I told her not to worry about me, "I own the bullet with MY name on it so I can never be shot with it!" She just looked at it and shook her head at my nonsense.

I guess I did it for it to be a cute little joke, but for some reason, I kept that .38 caliber cartridge throughout my law enforcement career. I saw it every day on top of my jewelry box as I was putting my uniform on. It was a personal reminder to always heed my mom's warning to "be careful out there."

I guess it must have worked because I was careful and I survived all those years during my career without being shot. I was in many scuffles, I got stabbed, and I once got shot AT on duty. But I never actually got shot - thanks to my mom's good advice and the good Lord above watching over me.

My mom has been gone for a long time now. But I still have that un-fired .38 cartridge with my name on it all these years later. I consider it just as valuable as the jewelry and watches that shares space with it in the jewelry box. Now, it serves less as a reminder for me to be careful, and more of a daily acknowledgement of my mom's undying love for me.

Blue Light Special

While on the subject of my parents, I blame my father for my love of pranks. After all, he's the one who gave me a giant sparkler and a box of matches when I was a kid and watched with glee as I tried again and again to light it and failed. It turned out to be a welding rod.

Sometimes when I would accompany him to construction jobs, he would delight in sending me to ask one of the other workers to borrow a left-handed hammer or some other nonsensical tool. So it stands to reason that when I heard about this prank to play on other officers, I was all-in!

I can't even remember who the deputy was who taught me this but it obviously had been filed away in my head. The patrol cars we were issued at the time had a single blue light atop the car. The rotating light itself was actually white, but the blue plastic lens that attached to the base made it appear blue in color. The blue plastic lens was held on by a simple buckle system. There was a metal collar/buckle system that went around the lens and the base of the light and buckled tightly to hold it all together – even at high rates of speed. Even though it was secure at high rates of speed, it was easy to quickly remove.

The premise of the prank was to catch one of your buddies busy out on a call or taking a bathroom break, steal his blue lens, and then hide somewhere close by to watch his reaction when he came out and found it missing. OK, I didn't say it was a great prank, but it was something mischievous to do on those slower nights. I had the occasion to pull this gag on a couple different deputies. The result was always better when they didn't know about the prank and thought they might have lost it somewhere along the highway on their way to the call they were on. Ahhh, good times.

Not exactly a prank, but while on the topic of blue lights, I want to share this. My brother Gary told me that when he first started in law enforcement there was a deputy that thought it would be a good idea to replace the bulb in the "bubblegum light" with an aircraft landing light. The idea was to make the single blue light brighter and more easily seen by other drivers and the people who he pulled over.

This did in fact make the light brighter, but when the deputy who made this modification got out on a prolonged call with the overhead going, there was an unforeseen problem.

The deputy who came up with this "brilliant" idea failed to factor in the intense heat created by an aircraft landing light bulb. The heat melted the pretty blue lens cover into an ugly blue blob on top of his patrol car. His supervisors were not amused.

BRAND NEW DISPATCHERS!

So, one of my coworkers had made an arrest and transported his prisoner to book in at the jail in Bartow. When he got back to our area of the county, we met up to chit-chat.

During the course of our conversation, he mentioned to me that he had stopped by communications to say hello. He knew that I was now a bachelor and might be interested to know some news he had learned while visiting communications. Two new cute dispatchers had been hired and this was their first day at work. I was definitely interested because I had been experiencing a bit of a dry spell in the dating department for a few months. I told him the next time I'm in Bartow, I'll stop in and check them out.

I didn't have to wait long. The very next day, I made a warrant arrest and booked the guy in at the jail. Remembering what my buddy had told me, I wandered over to communications to meet these two new girls. To this day, I can't tell you what one of them looked like because the first one I saw was absolutely stunning. She received ALL of my focus and attention that day because I thought she was absolutely beautiful.

Her name was Lynn. She spoke with the sweetest southern belle accent I had ever heard. She was slim, had short, dark, curly hair and was so cute that I honestly thought to myself, "she's way out of my league." I could tell right away that unlike the other girls that I had known up to this point, this one, this one was special.

This was only her second day on the job. She was being trained on teletype. The teletype operator was a specialized dispatcher who operated on a different channel and used the teletype to run tags, wanted person checks, and get warrant confirmations for the deputies back in the day. She was being trained by an older dispatcher named Perky. Perky said, "Hey Dale, show Lynn your 'S'!" I noticed the look of concern and confusion on Lynn's face.

As I began to unbutton the front of my uniform shirt, Lynn wasn't sure where all this was going. She was very shy and seemed so innocent and began to blush. After getting my uniform shirt opened, I grabbed each side of the shirt and spread it apart revealing the big super hero 'S' patch that I had hot glued to the front of my Kevlar vest for a laugh. Everyone in the room got a chuckle from it. Lynn was slightly embarrassed and was blushing even more - which endeared me to her even more-so.

I left communications and went back across the county and met up with my buddy who had told me about the two new dispatchers. I talked non-stop about Lynn and I think he could tell that I was infatuated.

I had to see her again – but outside of work. I let several days go by and called her on the phone to see if she would meet me for coffee somewhere. I set the meet date for a day I knew we were both off work. She turned me down. She was in college and said she had a test coming up that she had to study for. I was bummed out but said, "OK, maybe another time."

I thought about her constantly for several days. I saw another opportunity to get to know her better. Most of the deputies on our shift and the dispatchers were planning a shift get-together at a nice restaurant/bar after work in Lakeland. We were all on the 3:00 to 11:00 PM shift so the get-together wouldn't really get going until about 12:00 AM. If I was in my driveway right at the end of shift, I could quickly change clothes, hop into the Fiero, drive an hour to get there and make it by midnight. Tight schedule!

I called Lynn up and asked her if she planned to go to the shift get-together. She said, "I don't think so." I said, "Aww, c'mon, it'll be fun and we can get to know each other better." After a couple more pleads from me, she finally relented and said OK. Finally! I had a date with her - well, sort of. The whole shift was going to be there but at least I could see her again and we could chat.

Now the last thing I wanted to do was be late to this first date with my dream girl. I didn't want to get stuck out on a call at the last minute. So, I devised a plan. About 10:40 PM, I would find something to do that would take up about 10 minutes like a bar walk-through, or check out with a suspicious person if I could find one. As fate would have it, I found something even better. At least I thought it was better at the moment.

I happened to get behind a vehicle with a tag light that was burned out. I decided to stop the driver, kill a little time chatting with him, and let him off with a warning to get the tag light repaired.

I called in the tag number and informed the dispatcher that I was stopping the vehicle and where we were. I walked up to the door of his car and did the standard, "Do you know why I stopped you sir?" routine. The guy hung his head and said, "yes sir, the license plate doesn't belong to this car." I thought to myself, "Oh no, I'm going to have to issue him a ticket and this is going to seriously delay me if I don't hurry." I said, "do you know what else I stopped you for?" hoping that he would admit to knowing the tag light was burned out. Instead, he sighed and said, "yes sir. The car is stolen." I couldn't believe what I was hearing!

There was no way now that I was going to make my date. Tempting fate I said, "what else?" He said, because the tools in the back are stolen." "Anything else?" I asked timidly. "Yes sir, I have a warrant for my arrest." As it turned out, he had several warrants for his arrest. One in-county warrant and two out of state warrants. All of this added up to a mound of paperwork and at least three or four hours of my time getting the car towed, inventorying the vehicle's contents, logging the tools into evidence, writing the affidavits and report, and getting him booked into the jail.

Cell phones weren't even a thing back then. I had no way of contacting Lynn to tell her that I wouldn't be able to make our first date because of this mess that I had stumbled into right at the end of my shift. From Lynn's perspective, she was at a get-together where she barely knew anyone and the one person who had cajoled her to attend the event had stood her up. I thought to myself, "you really blew it this time Dale!"

The next afternoon, I called her and profusely apologized to her. I explained what had happened, but I couldn't get a read on how she felt about it. She was most likely still pretty upset with me. I tried to arrange another date with her but she again said she had a project due for college. Was I ever going to get to go out with this girl!?

Eventually, we did go out to dinner and after the rough start, I thought I could see a reciprocal spark in her eyes when she would look back at me. But I had competition. A Lieutenant with the Sheriff's Office (I'll call him "Lt. Dick" for the purposes of this book) could travel pretty much anywhere in the county he wished. Consequently, he could also stop in at communications any time he wanted to.

He saw the same beauty in Lynn that I did and begun to pressure Lynn to go out with him. He used his position of power to exert that pressure and eventually, since we were not mutually exclusive, she agreed to go out for coffee with him in hopes that it would satisfy him and he would hopefully leave her alone. It didn't work and he continued to pressure her for another date. She explained to him that she was kind of seeing me and preferred to not allow things to progress any further with him.

So, did he just let things drop there and move on? Nope. I should probably mention at this point that Lt. Dick wasn't just a random Lieutenant at the Sheriff's Office. He was MY lieutenant. He was my direct supervisor, just above my sergeant in my chain of command.

Lynn and I continued to see each other now on a more regular basis. I was definitely in love – although I had not spoken those words yet to Lynn. Several weeks passed and one day, Lt. Dick called me on the radio to meet with him in a strip-mall parking lot.

I pulled in next to his patrol car facing the opposite direction – driver's window to driver's window. After a couple minutes of small talk, he said, "I want to talk to you about Lynn." "What about her?" I asked. "I'm interested in her and I understand that you have been seeing her." "Yes sir, that is true" I said. "Well, I want you to shut it down," he said. I replied with stunned silence. He continued, "just tell her you're not interested in her anymore and you don't want to see her again." Again, my response was stunned silence.

This guy was my boss! I couldn't very well tell him to go to Hell. But at the same time, I was thinking in my head, "there is absolutely no way on God's green Earth that I am going to stop seeing this dream girl of mine just because he told me to!"

"Well, what do you say?" he asked. As I started to reply, the radio crackled to life breaking the silence as dispatch was calling me to send me on a theft in progress call. As I drove away, I shouted, "we'll talk later!" We never did. At least not about that topic.

I had never been so happy to be dispatched to a hot-call in all of my career as I was at that very moment. I fumed about his audacity for days. I was more resolved now than ever before to keep seeing Lynn.

Chapter 8 - WHICH FORMS DO I USE WHEN I SHOOT A MAN?

Another day at work. Things had been relatively quiet until I was sent to this late afternoon call. It was another domestic disturbance.

I had been to this couple's home on two other occasions for similar calls. They were one of those couples that just couldn't get along. Their anger, usually exacerbated by alcohol, would flair up and one of them would inevitably call the Sheriff's Office on the other one.

I pulled up in front of their house and walked up to the front door. The lady of the house met me at the door and said Leroy was drunk and causing problems again. On this visit, she seemed pretty lucid and wasn't drunk as a skunk like she had been on the few times I had responded there before. "He busted the mirror in the hall!" she said. I asked her where Leroy was at the moment. She said, "he's around back." I told her, "Wait here and I'll go talk to him."

I stepped away from the front door and began walking around back. I was cutting through their cluttered carport and was about in the center of it when Leroy came around the corner from the back yard. He was VERY agitated and intoxicated this time. That fact didn't concern me however as much as the fact that he had a two by four about four feet long in his hands. He was approaching me in a threatening manner with the two by four, holding it like a baseball bat.

In the police academy, we were taught something called "The Twenty-One Foot Rule." This "rule" was developed as a guideline for police officers from research conducted by a Salt Lake City, Utah Police Department instructor. His theories and research were taught in police academies nationwide.

According to his research, a person charging toward you with a knife or other blunt weapon, can travel twenty-one feet and use their weapon on you in the time it would take you to recognize the threat, draw your firearm, and fire two shots.

Leroy was right at that twenty-one-foot limit. Falling back on my training I drew my service revolver, a Model 629 and took aim at Leroy's center mass. I screamed at Leroy, "Drop the two by four" as I shuffled backwards a few feet. He took another step toward me with the two by four still raised in a striking position. Again, I shuffled backward a few more feet. But now, my back was up against the clutter and stacked boxes that were stored on their carport. Again, I shouted, "put down the two by four!"

Leroy took yet another step toward me and was now within about six feet of me. If you count the two by four, he was within about two to three feet of being able to inflict some serious injuries. I still clearly remember beginning to squeeze the trigger of my gun. I vividly remember seeing the hammer of the pistol beginning its journey backward. It was only a fraction of a second before the hammer was going to fall, firing the gun and sending 158 grains of hollow-point ammunition into this man's chest!

It's weird what goes through your mind in a situation like this. You might guess that fear was going through my mind. But it wasn't. I remember as I was watching the hammer come back in what seemed like slow motion, silently wondering to myself, "which report forms am I going to need to fill out when this is over?" I had never shot a man before so this was a new type of call for me. I thought to myself, "I'm going to need a person form, a narrative form, and of course an evidence form to book the two by four in as evidence." Then I thought, "I'll need to call an ambulance and my supervisors out here because when a law enforcement officer has to use his firearm in the line of duty, it's always a big deal! Then, I'll need to try to render first aid to Leroy until the ambulance gets here."

He moved toward me a bit more and one last time I shouted at him, "Leroy put down the stick!" Suddenly, he froze like a deer caught in headlights. He threw down the two by four! I'm not sure if he suddenly recognized me from the previous times I had been called to his residence or if it was the fact this last time, I had used his first name when I ordered him to drop his weapon. The hammer on my gun was almost all the way back and I'm sure if it had come back even a hair's width more, it would have fired. There's no doubt in my mind about that!

The danger from Leroy's make-shift weapon now over, I slowly lowered the hammer on the gun and ordered Leroy to turn around and put his hands behind his back. He complied and I arrested him on a number of charges without any further problems.

To this day, I'm sure Leroy doesn't know just how close he came to death that day. I don't know why he did what he did that day. I don't know why he decided to comply right at that last possible nano-second. Perhaps it was divine intervention.

As thankful as he should have been to be alive, I was equally thankful that I didn't have to take another person's life. It was only afterward that I felt fear or more accurately, anxiety regarding the whole thing. I thanked God that night during my prayers for saving both Leroy's life and me from having to deal with a life-time memory of killing someone. I'm still thankful even now - some forty years later.

Chapter 9 - A LONG RESPONSE TIME AND A ROMANTIC HORSE RIDE

Dirt roads and pastures

The area of the ridge that I worked was very rural. Frostproof was the name of the southern-most town in the county. It was a part of my assigned patrol area that I was probably the least familiar with.

I was working day shift on this particular day. I went outside my house in Lake Wales and hopped into my patrol car. I got on the radio, and informed dispatch that I was now in service and available for calls.

Almost immediately before I could even put my car in reverse to back out of the driveway, dispatch called me. "Bartow to 201, 10-65?" 10-65 was the code for, "can you pull over to write this down, we have a call for you." I answered in the affirmative and the dispatcher proceeded to give me an address in Frostproof. The call was to deliver a message to the resident – who didn't have a phone. The message was to contact her relative who lived out of state. It was in regards to a family emergency.

So, off I went bright and early toward Frostproof. The address was on a dirt road off another dirt road. People rarely put their addresses on their single-wide mobile homes in these rural areas and more often than not, street signs were down or missing completely. There were no GPS devices back then. We had to rely on a printed map book of the county to find addresses we were unfamiliar with and that map book was sometimes not up to date or accurate.

When I arrived in the general area, I began searching for the address they had sent me to. I diligently tried to find it to deliver the emergency message. I know if I had a family member that had died or was in dire medical distress, that I would appreciate the extra effort that I, as a deputy, was putting in to find them and deliver the message.

Try as I might, I couldn't find the address. I had been looking for an hour and a half when dispatch called me again. They had another call to send me on. I responded to that call and afterward, went right back to that remote area in Frostproof to look for the address again. No luck. Dispatch sent me on another call. After I cleared it, I again went back to the area in search of that address. This whole process continued to repeat itself all day long.

Finally at about ten minutes until 3:00 PM, I was back in the area searching one last time before going off duty and calling in that I was out of service for the day. I turned down a grass road. Notice I said a "grass road." It wasn't even a dirt road! Eureka! I found the mobile home.

I dutifully informed the resident of her family emergency and went on my way. She was thankful for me getting the message to her but she had no idea that it had taken me almost a full eight hours to find her house. That was the longest response time to a call I had during my entire career.

Upside down

While on patrol, one gets to meet a lot of people from many different walks of life. One sunny Saturday afternoon while out patrolling rural east Polk County, I saw a lady ride a horse up to her mailbox by the roadway to check her mail. I pulled over, rolled my window down, and said, "I like your mode of transportation there!" She chuckled and said she was out riding on her ranch anyway and thought she would stop and check her mail.

As I chatted with the lady, I thought to myself, "This would be a good romantic date activity to do with Lynn. Something totally unusual." The lady and I chatted for a little while longer and I asked her if she rented horses for people to ride and that I would love to take my girlfriend horseback riding. The lady said, "I don't rent them, but if you want to bring your girlfriend out, I would be happy to let y'all ride them for free." "That would be awesome!" I replied. I got her phone number and told her that I would be in touch.

I excitedly called Lynn on the phone and told her that I had something interesting to ask her that night when I saw her. I told her it was a date idea for us, but I didn't want to spill the beans until I saw her.

After I hung up with Lynn, I realized that I hadn't thought my plan completely through. You see, I had never ridden a horse before in my life. Well, there was a pony ride for my birthday when I was three or four years old, but watching westerns on TV was pretty much the only training I had ever had when it came to horses.

I thought to myself, "it's OK, Lynn will probably not be interested anyway and I'll be off the hook. She will probably prefer a nice dinner out somewhere instead." I said this to myself so many times on my way to pick her up for our date that I think I had convinced myself that she would say "no thanks" to going horseback riding or maybe she would forget that I had even mentioned a date idea to her. She didn't forget.

I pick her up and the first thing she says is, "so what's the big mystery date idea?" So much for her forgetting. I told her about the lady I had met and the offer to let us go horseback riding on her ranch. Lynn said "sounds like fun! I love horseback riding! When are we going to do it?"

Oh no! She was an experienced horseback rider. Now I was in deep! I had a date to go horseback riding with my girlfriend who I desperately wanted to impress, but just knew I would look like an absolute fool due to my lack of horsemanship.

I stuttered, "The lady said any time we want to go, I just need to call her and set up a date and time." Lynn said, "great! What about next weekend?" "OK" I replied. "I'll check back with her and set it up."

What to do, what to do!? I needed to learn how to ride a horse and I needed to learn FAST! That colorful fiberglass horse in front of the grocery store that takes quarters and goes around and around wasn't going to cut it. I needed real training on a real horse real fast!

I had a stroke of genius! I enlisted my fellow deputy, Tim Glower for help. Tim was in the Agriculture Unit (or a Citrus & Cattle Deputy) as we called them back then. Like me, Tim was a Lake Wales boy and we had become good friends. He would be able to help me!

Tim didn't have any horses, but he told me that his buddy, Gene Schmidt, a fellow Citrus and Cattle Deputy did! In fact, Gene was on the Sheriff's Posse – our agency's horse mounted patrol unit. I contacted Gene and explained my predicament. He said he'd be happy to teach me to ride.

I met Gene and he gave me some pointers and went over some basic things I needed to know, and up on his extra horse I climbed. We rode together through a big pasture at a relatively slow speed. Then, Gene thought we should pick up the pace a bit. I gently nudged the horse with my heels as Gene had instructed and true to form, my horse began to gallop! "This isn't so bad!" I thought to myself. "I'm doing it! I feel like a real cowboy!"

About thirty minutes later, Gene suggested we run them. I was game! Off we went, with Gene leading the way. I remembered what he had told me about slightly standing in the stirrups as the horse would run to let my knees act as shock absorbers.

The horses were in a full run in the slightly wooded area of his ranch. I noticed a low-hanging branch dead ahead of me. As I leaned over to keep it from smacking me in the face, I suddenly had a different viewpoint from the horse that was still in a full run.

My saddle had slipped around and I was now dangling upside down, hugging the horse's belly with my arms and legs as tightly as I could. All the while I'm thinking "If I let go, this is how I die. Trampled to death by a horse because I wanted to impress a girl!"

Fortunately, Gene looked back, noticed my distress, and slowed his horse and mine to a full stop. My legs were exhausted from holding on for dear life. I flopped like a bag of wet cement to the ground below my horse. I think the only thing louder than me flopping to the ground and attempting to catch my breath was the sound of laughter coming from Gene. What a day!

The next weekend rolled around and Lynn and I met the lady to go horseback riding. It went off (excuse the pun) without a hitch.

I do recall however, double checking before our ride to make sure that the saddle was securely cinched down tightly around the horse's middle. I felt like I rode that day like an experienced cowboy and I managed not to embarrass myself in front of my beautiful girlfriend. Yay for me!

Chapter 10 - A WHOLE NEW WORLD

I had worked the east side or "The Ridge" area of the county where I lived since being sworn in as a deputy. It was close to my mom's house where I was living and was in the area that I grew up in and was familiar with. I went to school there from elementary through high school. I knew most of the back roads and had become quite comfortable working that area.

One day, out of the blue, I got a memo in my inbox at the sub-station notifying me that I was being transferred to the Lakeland area effective immediately. Lakeland was on the opposite side of the county. The sub-station that I would be working out of was a good hour from my house.

I knew when I joined the Sheriff's Office that I could be assigned anywhere in the county they wanted to send me. I always knew that was a possibility. But in the back of my mind, I couldn't help but think that this transfer was initiated by Lt. Dick. So, I thought my best response to show him that it didn't bother me was to outwardly act joyful and happy about the transfer. And that's exactly what I did.

In retrospect, perhaps I WAS happy about it. I enjoyed working The Ridge, but to be honest, there were frequently times when there wasn't much action going on. Just a lot of patrolling cow pastures, orange groves, and pine trees. The change from being assigned to a rural area to a more densely populated city area could be fun. There were more calls, more excitement, and more deputies to get to know and become friends with. Other than the long commute to the sub-station for briefings and then again back home, this could be enjoyable. And you know what? It was!

The Sergeant I was assigned to was Tim Holly. He was a great supervisor and I really looked up to him and respected him. Still do. He was serious about his deputies getting the job done, but cool enough that he would cut-up with us and have fun.

I can't remember what inspired this, but he and I once before briefing, climbed on top of the sub-station's roof and posed for pictures as super heroes – much to the delight of the rest of the squad.

We had our hands on our hips in our best super hero pose and we wore riot helmets with clear face shields. Our bright yellow raincoats were used as our capes. We looked majestic! Tim called our crime-fighting duo characters "Deputy Dynamic & Special Friend!" I still have one of the pictures from that day. Tim was a hoot!

Is that a banana in your pocket?

One of the first deputies I met in Lakeland was named Dan Callet. He was a couple years older than me but we got along famously and became fast friends. Dan was throwing a costume party at his house on the weekend before Halloween and invited me to attend. Lynn was going to be working and wasn't able to go, so I accepted the invitation and planned to go solo. The party was about a week away so I had time to decide on a great costume to wear.

In Winter Haven, the town between Lake Wales where I lived and

Lakeland where I was now assigned, there was a costume rental shop. I had never spent money to rent a costume before, but I wanted something professionally made to wear. I wanted to make a good impression on my new Lakeland friends. I walked into the costume rental shop and was astonished at the selection of costumes that were available.

From the time I was a kid, I have always gravitated to non-scary or funny Halloween costumes. I didn't go in for the blood and gore stuff. I would much rather wear a costume that made people smile or that would give people a hearty laugh. As I wandered through the shop perusing all the costumes, one caught my eye!

A full gorilla costume with the mask, hands, feet, and furry body. I got excited! "I want THAT!" I exclaimed to the proprietor of the shop. He replied, "sorry, that one's already rented for Halloween." I told him, I didn't need it on Halloween, I need it on the weekend before Halloween." "Oh" he said, "well, then it's yours!" It was perfect and I was overjoyed!

While I was there taking care of the paperwork, I noticed some cans of "Silly String" on the counter by the cash register. A thought popped into my head about how to use it, so I bought a can.

I picked up the costume on the Friday before the party on Saturday. Friday night, I decided I should try everything on just to make sure it fit ok. It did! As I was standing in my bedroom looking at myself in the mirror in full gorilla regalia, I glanced down and noticed some clean laundry that I hadn't put away yet was lying on my bed. That's when this stroke of genius hit me!

What's funnier than a guy in a gorilla costume? A guy dressed as a gorilla wearing tighty-whitey underwear! I pulled on a pair of my underwear over the hairy gorilla costume and it looked absolutely ridiculous! Just the look I was going for!

I walked out in to the living room to show my mom. She was sitting in a chair facing away from me watching television. I sneaked up behind her and jumped into view gyrating my underwear-clad furry hips! It startled her at first and then she just shook her head, chuckled, and said, "boy, you ain't right!"

Fast forward to Saturday night. It was almost time for me to leave my house to attend the party. My buddy Charles pulled into the driveway and walked into the house. He wanted to hang out, but I told him that I was just about to leave for a costume party. Then I said, "hey, why don't you just come with me!?" He said, "but I don't have a costume." I replied, "that's ok, I'm sure there will be other people there who show up with no costume, it'll be fine!" He agreed and off we drove.

A few miles from Dan's house a thought occurred to me and I told Charles that I should probably not show up empty handed. We stopped at a convenience store and I told Charles to go in and buy a pack of wine coolers. (Wine coolers were popular back then, don't judge me!) He said, "why do *I* have to go in?" I replied, "look at me man! I'm dressed like a gorilla! Just go in and get the dang wine coolers." He obliged and went in to make the purchase.

As we drove the rest of the way to Dan's house – which I had only been to one time before in the daylight – I told Charles my plan. I explained I wanted to make a really BIG entrance! I wanted him to open the door for me, I would jump into the living room squirting Silly String everywhere while shouting "LET'S PARTY!"

We got into the neighborhood and I was a little confused. The houses all looked similar and like I said, I had only been there once before during the daytime. But I managed to find the house! There were cars parked up and down the street and in the yard so I knew I had the right place.

We got out of my car, I put on the gorilla mask, feet, and gloves and stuck a banana down the front of my tighty-whiteys for an extra laugh. I remember walking up the sidewalk and hearing the rubber gorilla feet slap against the concrete like I was wearing swim fins. Here's a public service announcement for you; rubber gorilla feet aren't made for walking in!

So, we get to the door, I readied the Silly String, and nodded to Charles to fling open the door! He did so and I jumped into the house as planned dressed as a gorilla wearing a banana in his under wear, waving a four-pack of wine coolers in one hand and squirting Silly String all over the party-goers with my other hand while shouting, "LET'S PARTY!"

Through the eye holes of the gorilla mask, I began to scan the crowd for someone I knew. It was only then that I realized not only were none of these people wearing costumes, they were sitting around in a circle. Most of them were holding bibles in their hands. I didn't see any familiar faces. I HAD GOT THE WRONG HOUSE!

I had burst in on some people who were in the middle of their bible study meeting wearing a ridiculous gorilla costume with a less than appropriate banana stuck down my underwear, carrying alcoholic beverages, and had just sprayed Silly String all over these poor people. After a long, awkward pause, one of them spoke up and said, "I think you want Dan Callet's house next door."

I could feel the heat from my embarrassed face reflecting back on me from the interior of the gorilla mask. My voice muffled by the mask I asked, "are you serious?" The man who had spoken up said, "I'm afraid so." I backed out of the house, shuffling those giant rubber gorilla feet backwards while saying, "I am so sorry." The last thing I saw before I closed the door was one of the bible study group members removing the Silly String that was hanging off of his eye glasses.

We went next door to Dan's actual house and I told Dan what had happened. He just chuckled and jokingly said, "great, now I'm going to have to move!" We all laughed.

This was probably one of the most embarrassing moments of my life. I'm so glad my face was completely concealed by that mask so they couldn't see how red it was from embarrassment. I would be willing to bet that the folks who were at that get together still talk about the time their bible study got crashed by a partying gorilla wearing nothing but his underwear.

Chapter 11 – A PEANUT AND A SHOTGUN

Peanut and Boom-Boom

I hadn't been assigned to the Lakeland area long before a tragedy struck. It happened at night in the northern most part of that side of the county in a small town called Polk City.

The report was that a man had been hit by a train and I was being temporarily sent the next morning when it became daylight to Polk City to assist other deputies, detectives, and crime scene techs. When I arrived, I was told that the man hit by the train was likely sleeping on the track when the accident occurred. Now you may be asking yourself, who in their right mind would sleep on a railroad track. Well, nobody. This guy wasn't in his right mind. He was mentally challenged. I don't remember his actual name, but his nickname was "Peanut."

Peanut was a local who didn't really get arrested a lot, but had a lot of interactions with law enforcement. He would walk in the roadway impeding traffic or he would annoy people at the convenience store or the feed store when he would pan-handle them and get the law called on him. When told to move along, he always complied.

I was partnered with another deputy, John Cokely, and was given an evidence bag. We were both assigned to walk along each side of the track for about a mile and a half or so and collect any of Peanut's body parts that we could find.

The wheels of the train had chopped up Peanut pretty bad. We were told not to be too concerned with small bits of entrails and to collect only body parts. My one big find was a finger. It may have been a toe. It was a little difficult to distinguish which one it actually was. All along the track there were bits of Peanut's entrails and his blood.

At one point, for some reason, I glanced behind where John and I were walking and about fifty yards back, I saw another individual. It was a female civilian and she seemed to be walking along, looking at the ground just like we were.

She would occasionally stop and collect something off the ground. I asked John whose regular patrol assignment was the Polk City area, "who is that!?" He looked back at her and said, "oh, that's Boom-Boom. That's Peanut's girlfriend. She's not right in the head either." He continued, "I guess we should tell her to get off the track and leave the area while we search."

We walked up to Boom-Boom and she had a small, dirty rag doll in her hands. It was about ten inches tall and looked like it had seen its better days. John asked Boom-Boom, "what are you doing out here?" She parted a split in the fabric of the rag doll and pulled out a Zip-lock bag with tiny bits of Peanut's bloody entrails in it. She happily said, "I'm getting Peanut's innards for my Peanut doll. Peanut doesn't need them anymore since he's in Heaven now."

John told her we're still conducting our investigation and she needed to get away from the railroad track. "Maybe you can come back out tomorrow" he said. She happily complied and literally skipped down the road that ran along-side the tracks, back toward town. John and I continued our search but didn't speak of Boom-Boom the rest of the time we were searching. I thought about her though.

I thought about her the rest of the time I was searching and periodically over the last 40 years. I thought about how Boom-Boom didn't seem sad or upset, yet seemed to understand exactly what had happened to Peanut.

I've contemplated on it a lot and figure that making that "Peanut doll" was her way of grieving the loss of her boyfriend. It's a sad story at first glance, but if you think about it, it's a life lesson for us all as well. The lesson is this; It's OK to mourn the loss of a loved one in whatever manner that is right for us individually. However, we should all be happy and rejoice in the thought that they are now in a better place. It took a simpleton to teach me this insightful lesson. God works in mysterious ways.

Crap! That's a shotgun!

I was on the graveyard shift. It was about 2:00 AM and I had just polished off a thirty-two-ounce soda I had bought at a convenience store when the radio suddenly crackled to life. Dispatch was sending my buddy Ed, an older deputy, probably in his early 50's, to a domestic disturbance in progress call. After they dispatched him, they called me and sent me as a secondary for back up.

As a law enforcement officer, domestic disturbance calls become pretty routine. However, they can also be VERY dangerous. You just never know what the situation is going to be when you arrive. Will those involved be compliant and settle down? Or, will they be combative and violent?

We arrived in front of the residence about the same time. It was an older neighborhood on a quiet street. We both got out of our patrol cars and after a pleasantry, began walking side by side up the walkway leading to the front door. There was a short hedge about two feet high that lined each side of the sidewalk. From inside the residence, we could hear a male voice screaming at what was later determined to be his wife. Suddenly, I heard the sound of glass breaking. My eyes immediately went to the source of the sound, a window to the left side of the front door.

I instantly saw what had broken the window. It was the barrel of a shotgun and it was aimed right down the middle of the sidewalk toward Ed and me! I shouted, "GUN!" and without even thinking about it, shoved Ed to one side as I leaped across the short hedge on the opposite side of the walkway. We both landed on our bellies just as the shotgun fired a blast right down the center of the sidewalk.

We hurriedly scampered away, low-crawling our separate directions in search of cover. I don't know exactly where Ed went, but I found a nice solid oak tree to take cover behind. I heard Ed call for additional units to back us up.

Several minutes passed and the front door slammed open. It was the man's wife and she was holding an infant in her arms. I left my position of cover to grab her and guide her to safety a few houses down the street. Her friend lived there and allowed her to come in.

I returned to my position behind the tree. I could hear multiple sirens coming to our aid in the distance. A supervisor asked us our position over the radio and told us to back away further from the suspect's house but to maintain visual. I crossed the street and found a neighbor's hedge to hide behind. It didn't provide me cover, but since it was very dark that night, it provided me concealment. There was no way for the suspect to see me where I was hidden.

Within a few minutes, a dozen or more deputies had arrived and were taking up perimeter positions around the house and surrounding neighborhood streets. From my position about 50-60 yards away, I could see the suspect's front door, side yard, and part of his back yard. It was a good spot.

We had a barricaded subject and now, it was a waiting game. The Lieutenant on scene instructed dispatch to call out our SWAT team. I knew it was going to take a while for SWAT to arrive. As I laid behind that hedge in the darkness, I felt an overwhelming urge to urinate.

From the time I was very little and playing hide-and-go-seek, I can remember getting the urge to pee while I was hiding. I can't be the only one who experiences this. Perhaps even you, the person reading this, has the same issue. The problem I had this time, was that there was no place to go. Plus, I needed to maintain my position since I could see so much of the house and report suspect movement if need be.

I couldn't hold it any longer. I decided I needed to pee RIGHT NOW! So, I devised a plan! I rolled several times, remaining behind the hedge and while still on my side, relieved myself on the ground. When I finished, I quickly rolled back to my original spot just in case my newly made pee puddle decided to migrate toward me. I made it! I got to pee and remained dry in the process!

Just then, I heard movement behind me. It was a sergeant that worked the Lakeland area. Nobody really cared for this guy. He had a really abrasive personality. He low-crawled up next to me and asked, "Seen any movement on this side?" I replied, "no, I haven't seen anything, but it sounds like he's in there breaking up furniture and dishes."

As I was talking, I realized that the sergeant was lying right in the spot where I had just peed. I started to say something, but I didn't. I figured, "what the heck. This guy has a "pissy" attitude, he might as well smell the part!" I silently chuckled to myself. He said, "OK, let us know if you see anything." "Yes sir," I responded.

About an hour went by. SWAT was on scene and had the power cut to the neighborhood. With all the house lights and street lights now off, it was even darker than before. The suspect had brought several arm-loads of furniture, the wife's clothing, and other items into the back yard. He piled everything up and lit them on fire. Then, I watched as he opened the tailgate of his pick-up, leaned his shotgun against the truck, and took a seat on the tailgate to watch the bonfire he had created.

As he sat there on the back of the pick-up, drinking a beer and watching the flames, I watched an amazing sight unfold. SWAT team members came from everywhere! Some dropped out of a nearby tree, some came around the corner of the house, one rolled out from underneath the back of the truck the suspect was sitting on! It was amazing to see them swarm the guy in such a coordinated manner. The guy was just as surprised as I was. They were all able to take him into custody without another shot being fired. An exciting, memorable night on the job for sure!

Chapter 12 - OPERATION PURITY

Lynn and I were married in a church wedding in her hometown of Fort Meade, Florida. Dispatcher Vickie Barry was one of Lynn's maids of honor. Dispatcher Rita Lorrance did Lynn's hair and make-up. Three of my deputy friends, John Cokely, Dan Callet, and Lanny Sharefield attended the wedding. John Cokely acted as one of my groomsmen. It was like a work reunion! I have no idea how we were all able to be off at the same time for the wedding.

It poured rain during the ceremony. In fact, it was more of a deluge. According to Hindu traditions and lore, rain on your wedding day is good luck because it signifies that your marriage will last. As you know, a knot that becomes wet is extremely hard to untie – therefore, when you "tie the knot" on a rainy day, your marriage is supposedly just as hard to unravel!

I got along great with Lynn's parents, Gene who owned his own welding business was an auxiliary deputy for the Sheriff's Office and a fellow firearms enthusiast. Her mother, Lela, worked at the public library in Fort Meade. They loved me and always treated me more like a son than a son-in-law.

Things were going well! Lynn moved out of the house she was living in in Lakeland with her roommate Vickie Barry and we moved into our own apartment in Winter Haven. She eventually left the Sheriff's Office and went to work at the Winter Haven Police Department as a dispatcher. She joined my brother Carl at WHPD who was already working there as a patrolman. She was doing great at her new department and was one of the first dispatchers in our county to become a "911 certified" dispatcher.

Earlier in this book, I mentioned the new Sheriff, Dan Dumasse, who had been elected. Almost immediately after being elected, Sheriff Dumasse begun implementing department policies that made a lot of people raise their eyebrows. He was often openly critical of blacks and other minorities. And he was rumored to have been a high-ranking member of the Ku Klux Klan.

One of his many blunders as Sheriff was his mismanagement of Sheriff's Office funds. Because of his own doings, he found the department in serious financial straits. His solution was to cut manpower and fire personnel. That was yet another poor decision considering that we always seemed to be shorthanded as it was.

He cloaked this scheme in a name that he thought would garner public acceptance and approval. He called it, "Operation Purity." His suggestion was that the department had employees who were under-performing cops, people who were not pulling their weight, or had become discipline problems.

He went to his front-line Lieutenants and demanded they provide him names of deputies under their command who they thought needed to be terminated as part of Operation Purity in order to "Purify" the Sheriff's Office.

A lot of good deputies were terminated in this fiasco. Some with only months to go until their retirements. Almost twenty deputies over all were fired! Everyone was walking on eggshells. Every day we would come to work and hear about another few deputies getting fired for no apparent reason. It wasn't funny, but it kind of became a running joke. When we would walk into briefing it was like, "well, who got "Purified" today?" One dayshift, it was my turn.

I had been humping calls all morning and was called by dispatch to return to the Lakeland sub-station. Once I arrived, I was informed by a Sergeant that I was being terminated. He was very empathetic but couldn't tell me a reason. Nobody could. In fact, if you were to go to the Sheriff's Office today and pull my personnel file, the last page, the termination page, actually says at the bottom, "Reason for termination: UNKNOWN."

My job performance was stellar and I'm convinced that my name was not just randomly pulled out of a hat. I mentioned the Sheriff went to his front-line Lieutenants for name suggestions of who they thought should be fired. Lieutenant Dick, my supervisor when I was still working the Ridge was one of the people he asked for suggestions. Of course, Lieutenant Dick saw this as the ultimate way to get back at me for not giving up on dating Lynn. It was a golden opportunity for him to exact his revenge on me and ruin my career.

The same sergeant that was tasked with telling me I was officially terminated was also tasked with riding with me in my patrol car to my apartment in Winter Haven where, standing in my own living room, he inventoried all my uniforms, badges, guns, and other equipment I had been issued. He then packed the equipment into my patrol car and drove away.

I was emotionally crushed. It was devastating. I was gutted. My life-long dream job had been snatched away from me in an instant. I sat down on the couch, stunned and in disbelief about what had just happened to me. I didn't know what to do. I sat there by myself in silence for what must have been an hour. My head was spinning.

I drove my Fiero up to the Winter Haven Police Department to break the news to Lynn. This wasn't something to tell her over the phone. She too was shocked and disappointed. She felt sorry for me. She knew how much my career in law enforcement meant to me.

A few deputies and I contacted an attorney to sue Dan Dumasse and the Sheriff's Office for wrongful termination. But after researching it, sadly, the lawyer informed us that there was nothing we could do because of the way Florida law was written at the time. Basically, the law stated that, "deputies serve at the pleasure of the Sheriff." Meaning that he fired us and there was absolutely no recourse for us.

I admit that I shed a few tears about this whole mess. I knew I was a good deputy. I worked circles around my older co-workers. I had received commendations for several calls that I handled. I was always eager to take a call. I knew I wasn't "lazy" or "dead wood." I had never been written up or disciplined for any reason. I was a good employee. Lieutenant Dick had won the battle by getting me fired. But Lynn married me. So, I feel like I was the one who had won the war.

My consolation came about a year and a half later. Sheriff Dumasse was forced to step down following a grand jury investigation that called for his resignation. It cited overwhelming evidence of misconduct and incompetence on the part of Sheriff Dan Dumasse and many of the people he had put in positions of leadership. Specifically, it criticized him for hiring two sergeants from the outside with previous proven ties to the Ku Klux Klan.

The grand jury also raised questions about how Dumasse handled the Sheriff's Office budget and allegations that he paid civilian groups with some of the agency's funds. The grand jury report also accused him of bid-rigging. All of this was documented and chronicled in the Lakeland newspaper and through other media outlets.

What goes around comes around Dumasse!

Chapter 13 - MORE MONKEY BUSINESS

With my dream job in law enforcement stolen from me, I was feeling pretty low. I took a job at a local theme park, Cypress Gardens, as a security officer. They hired me almost instantly because of my Sheriff's Office background. They didn't even seem to mind that I had been terminated as part of Operation Purity. I think by that time, everyone in the county had figured out that Sheriff Dumasse was just an incompetent buffoon.

Initially, I worked on day shift. About three months later, they had the person in charge of the midnight shift retire. They moved me to midnight shift and because of my law enforcement background, put me in charge of the shift. I had three guys under me. We all became great friends and as dead and boring as midnight shift in a small theme park was, you can imagine that it wasn't long before the shenanigans started.

After our rounds, we would play flashlight tag on the golf carts in one of the darkest areas of the park, the botanical gardens. If you got a flashlight shined on you, you had to sit still for thirty seconds and then you were "it." And the game continued. It was a fun game, but it also incentivized my guys to patrol an area of the park that was often neglected.

Sometimes, during our lunch break, I would let them all go for a twenty-minute swim in the huge "Aquacade Pool" where high-dive shows were performed during the daytime for the tourists.

It was fun and provided a team building and bonding experience for them. The guys loved it and they loved having me as their supervisor. On my nights off, I even took Lynn and my nephew, Alan for late night swims in the big "show pool."

While I was employed at Cypress Gardens, they constantly would run national television ads for the park featuring what had become the unofficial mascot of Cypress Gardens. It was a monkey named "Sampson." Sampson became quite a star and was recognized by park visitors immediately. He was a bona-fide celebrity!

Sampson lived on an "island" with a harem of girl monkeys. The island was surrounded by a mote and a four-foot concrete wall that guests could walk right up to and take pictures of the big star.

One night, one of my security officers, Jim Saladais, and I were standing there and I made some wisecrack joke. Jim slapped my shoulder. Sampson came unglued! He started screeching and jumping around his little island. After he calmed down a bit I said, "let's try it again. Grab my shoulder and shake me like you're hurting me and let's see what he does." Jim shook my shoulder and sure enough, Sampson went (excuse the pun) ape again.

We tried it the other way around with me shaking Jim, but it elicited no response from the monkey whatsoever. I figured out why. As a security guard, I had keys to every building in the park. One of those buildings was the facility where they readied food for all of the various animals exhibited in the park.

I love animals so much that almost every night while making my rounds, I would stop by that building and get a small container full of large purple grapes to toss to Sampson and his girlfriends.

They LOVED those grapes. I surmise that Sampson saw me as a friend. A person who supplied him with a midnight snack of sweet tasty grapes every night and he just didn't appreciate somebody messing with his "meal ticket."

A few weeks later, I was working with a different guard and decided to show him how Sampson reacted any time someone appeared to be hurting me. We stopped by the animal building first to grab some grapes and then off to Sampson's Island we went.

I spent some time pitching grapes to Sampson and the other monkeys and then told the other guard to grab my shoulder and shake me as if he was trying to hurt me. The instant before he did so, I looked over at Sampson and he had just popped a grape into his mouth. He saw what he perceived as someone fighting me and started to monkey scream at them. But then suddenly, he grabbed his own little throat. He wasn't making a sound! Oh my God! He was choking to death on a grape! I felt awful!

I panicked! I actually considered hopping the wall and wading through the mote to the island to try to save him. Thank goodness good sense prevailed. Two thoughts crossed my mind. One, I had never given a monkey a Heimlich maneuver before. And two, monkeys can be vicious when they get excited. I didn't know how Sampson or his girlfriends might react.

So, we just watched in helpless horror and talked about how we were going to explain to the big bosses that we had killed the parks most famous attraction!

Thankfully, somehow, Sampson dislodged the grape and was ok. On other occasions, I showed other security guards how Sampson would react when he thought someone was hurting me, but after that harrowing incident, I always made it a point to give him the grapes AFTER my demonstration.

CHAPTER 14 - THE MAGIC IS BACK!

So THAT is how it works

When I was on dayshift at Cypress Gardens, I always planned my rounds to coincide with the start time of the live magic show they had at the "Magic Lantern Theater." I still loved the art of theatrical magic and thoroughly enjoyed watching the magicians perform their shows. I saw it so many times, I almost knew the show by heart. Watching the magic performances rekindled the fire inside of me to perform magic shows again myself – especially since my career at the Sheriff's Office ended abruptly.

After I was promoted to midnight shift supervisor, I spent time by myself looking and snooping around backstage at the magic show. There was one illusion they did in the show that confounded me. And I decided to figure out how it worked. When I went to work that night, the theater was shut down for refurbishing. All of the illusions, magic tricks, and stage props were gone! "Oh well" I thought to myself, "maybe not knowing the secret is a good thing. It keeps the sense of wonder alive."

Not too far from where the theater was located, stood a mansion on property. The exterior was finished like a southern plantation mansion from yesteryear. The inside housed a few Cypress Gardens business offices and was used for storage for seasonal decorations and such.

Late one night, I was in the mansion performing my security duties and spotted all the equipment from the magic show stored there – including the illusion that I wanted so badly to know the secret to. I opened the illusion to see it's inner workings and saw – NOTHING! I must have examined every corner and edge of that illusion both inside and out, to find out how it was accomplished. I found nothing suspicious.

Exasperated at my own inability to figure it out, I leaned on part of the door of the illusion for support and a secret panel opened. Initially, I thought I had broken it! But soon, I realized I had discovered the methodology behind the magic trick. I was a little disappointed to know the secret and thrilled to know the secret all at the same time. The experience lit a fire under me to get my own new show together and begin performing again!

I went home and told Lynn my plan. Since being a magician was all that I really knew other than law enforcement, it was a perfect side hustle. I could do magic shows in the evening and on weekends and still keep my midnight shift job in security! It was a perfect plan! And that's exactly what I did!

As I continued to perform shows in addition to the security job, I poured any extra income we had back into building my show up to make it bigger and better. Eventually, one of the props I added to my show was the same magic illusion that had confounded me and that I had accidentally stumbled upon the secret to in the mansion that night.

Birds of a feather

Magic is a small world. Magicians enjoy hanging out together, sharing tips and tricks and networking with one another. There are magician's conventions held every year across the nation and local magic clubs where they congregate monthly. It is at these magic clubs where I met several people who became life-long friends – even to this day!

I found out that I didn't have to travel far to find a magic club. There was one that met every month in Bartow. Lynn and I began attending regularly and it's where I met Scott Huston, a young seventeen-year-old kid who had a passion for magic that reminded me of my own when I was young. Since then, Scott grew up and has made magic his career. He currently tours nationwide performing school assemblies and for churches.

I met Tommy Jason. Tommy was and is one of the finest card magicians I know. Some magicians specialize in a specific genre of magic and card tricks were Tommy's specialty. Tommy holds a world record for distance in "Card Scaling." Card Scaling is the art of throwing standard playing cards with great accuracy or force. It is performed both as part of stage magic shows and as a competitive physical feat among magicians, with official records existing for longest distance thrown, fastest speed, highest throw, greatest accuracy, and the greatest number of cards in one minute. Tommy was also a magician at The Magic Lantern Theater at Cypress Gardens, but he worked there before I started in security.

I also met my running buddy, James Allard. I love James like a brother. His sense of humor is sharp as a tack. We spent so much time hanging out together that Lynn started calling our outings, "man dates." Being a comedian, one hears a lot of jokes and after a while, it's difficult to find things that'll make you laugh out loud. James has always been a person who makes that happen for me. He is one funny guy! I could write a whole other book about the shenanigans he and I have gotten into over the years.

Kelly Forner is another amazing guy I met at the Bartow magic club. He performed with live doves and he later influenced me to do the same. Kelly is one of the most friendly, amicable, and supportive friends I have.

Last but certainly not least, I met Doug Andrews. Doug was a cruise ship magician. I found out that he lived in Winter Haven. Ironically just before performing cruise ships full time, he was also one of the magicians who performed the shows at Cypress Gardens! He left to begin his cruise ship career shortly before I started working there in security. Doug has traveled the world performing his magic on ships. Today, he's retired from cruise ships, but still accepts gigs in and around his home state of Oklahoma. Doug is another really funny man that makes me laugh out loud!

I continued to perform locally for birthday parties and civic organizations and decided I should expand my networking. I discovered that there was a large magic club located in the much larger city of Orlando. Orlando was only about forty-five minutes to an hour's drive away so once a month, it was easily doable.

It was at the Orlando magic club where I met another guy whose humor is razor sharp. Fred Moorse is that very funny friend. Fred, also a cruise ship performer has parlayed his magic career into being one of the leading public speakers on time management for the corporate world. Fred was and still is what I consider one of my best friends and I cherish that friendship very much.

I love humor and one of the most important things I look for in a friend is an ability to make me laugh. All of the guys I have mentioned above – and many others – have elicited much laughter from me over the years and I hope I have returned the favor to them.

After making all these new contacts, my show grew even more. I added more magic effects, sound equipment, fog machines, lighting, and backdrops to the show to transform it from a simple magic show into a theatrical experience. I began accepting more corporate gigs which meant higher pay. Between my job in security and my magic show side-hustle I was making more than what I was earning as a deputy sheriff.

I was torn in two directions career-wise. I wanted to go full time into the entertainment business, but I yearned to be back in law enforcement. After being fired from a law enforcement agency, I didn't think any other department would touch me with a ten-foot pole.

I applied at the Tampa Police Department, Haines City Police Department, and the Winter Haven Police Department. Heck, I even considered learning Spanish and applying to be a Border Patrol officer. Soon, I would see light at the end of the tunnel.

CHAPTER 15 - THE PHOENIX RISES

A family affair

I was beginning to think that I was "damaged goods." That no agency wanted to hire me after being fired from the Sheriff's Office. But one Tuesday afternoon, I received a call that would change the course of my career life for the better!

Lieutenant Fred Deleon from the Winter Haven Police Department was on the other end of the line. He told me that he was in charge of personnel and new hires and was interested in interviewing me. This sort of surprised me since my older brother, Carl was already working there as a sworn officer and my wife Lynn was also working there as a dispatcher.

The whole interview, background, and polygraph exams all went extremely fast and I was hired! I was a law enforcement officer again! I was so grateful then and even to this day for Lieutenant Deleon seeing through the former sheriff's B.S. and for giving me a second chance at my dream job.

After only a year as a security officer, I bid my security team, supervisors, and Sampson the monkey at Cypress Gardens farewell. I am thankful Cypress Gardens provided me a job, or bridge if you will, until I found another job in law enforcement. I'm also thankful that because of Cypress Gardens, my love of magic and performing was awakened inside of me again.

It wasn't long after I started in patrol at W.H.P.D. that my sister-in-law Kelly, Carl's wife, was hired as a community service officer. Now the count of Garretts working there was up to FOUR! About a year later, my brother Gary joined the force followed later by his wife, Lindy. Wow! Now there were SIX Garretts all at one police department.

Captain J.J. Staten took a shine to all of us Garretts but he has admitted in more recent years that the administration always worried about the Garrets having a death in the family or some other type of family emergency. The concern was that it would pull a significant number of the work force away from our duties. Thankfully, that situation never arose.

Mistaken identity

Case #1: Being a police officer was pretty much a guarantee that at some point, you are going to upset a civilian by giving them a traffic citation or arresting them. My oldest brother, Gary, always struggled with keeping his anger in check. He has always been like that from the time I was little.

He had previously been a cop in the early 1970's. Things were different back then. People respected law enforcement much more than they do today. And if they decided to be drunk and combative, police were happy to oblige them in physical contact. The person acting out would typically go to jail with a few extra bumps and bruises than they started out with that morning.

Although Gary had attended the academy and learned the kinder, gentler ways of handling suspects and prisoners, he would occasionally slip back into that old cop mentality and come off as too authoritative or aggressive. This resulted in several complaints being filed against him. The exaggerated allegations against him were never really substantiated, yet every incident – no matter how minor - was placed in his personnel jacket.

My brother Carl was in court one day on a case he had been subpoenaed for but had no recollection of the arrestee or the case in general. The young defense attorney was firing questions at Carl left and right. "On the night of October 23rd you arrested my client and roughed him up, didn't you?" said the attorney. "No sir" replied Carl. "You've had several complaints of excessive force in the past, isn't that true?" Again, Carl responded, "no sir." The lawyer becoming visibly frustrated and angry himself said, "what about on December 5th last year?" Carl replied again, "No sir." What about March 28th of this year? Did you not have a complaint filed against you for using excessive force on that date?" Carl again replied, "no sir I did not."

Now very angry and feeling like he had caught Carl perjuring himself under oath said, "Take a look at these documents we obtained from your personnel file. Do these refresh your memory?" Again, Carl said, "no sir they don't."

Now, so angry and feeling like he had Carl dead to rights said, "are these not your signatures on the bottom of these documents?" Again, Carl said "no sir." So excited and angry that his head was about to explode, the lawyer said, "well if those aren't your signatures can you tell the people of the jury just whose signatures are at the bottom of these complaints!?"

Carl looked at them again even though it had already dawned on him what was going on. Then he looked up and said, "yes sir, those are my brother's signatures." Carl told me that you could see the attorney's body deflate in defeat and embarrassment. When he pulled the complaint reports he had paid too much attention to the last name and no attention to the first name. "Uh, No further questions your honor."

<u>Case #2:</u> Carl went up to the department off duty and in civilian clothes one day to pick up a copy of a report for another upcoming court appearance. After getting the report from our

records window, he sat down in the lobby to read over the report.

A citizen entered the lobby of the department and went up to the dispatcher window. Carl immediately recognized the citizen from the day before when he had given him a ticket for speeding. Carl recalled that the citizen was agitated during the traffic stop and he figured that the guy was going to be one of those people who hoped to help his case by marching down to the police department and filing a complaint against the "mean ole police officer" who had dared to write him a ticket. Sure enough, here he was in the police department's lobby to do just that.

Carl raised the report he was reading a bit higher concealing most of his face and surreptitiously listened to the exchange. The dispatcher said, "can I help you sir?" Clearly agitated, the man replied, "yes ma'am you can! I want to file a complaint on one of your officers!" The dispatcher asked, "ok, which officer do you want to complain on?"

The man said, "his name was officer Garrett!" The dispatcher looked at him and said, "ok, which one?" Even more agitated, the guy says "what do you mean which one?" The dispatcher remaining cool, calm, and collected says, "we have several Garretts that work here sir." "Well how many are there?" he asked. The dispatcher replied, "there are six Garrets that work here sir." The guy even more flustered, spun around on his heels and was heard as he was leaving in a huff through the front door say, "awww, just forget it!"

It was all Carl and the dispatcher, who had been in each other's line of sight the whole time, could do not to laugh. But, as soon as the front lobby door closed, they both shared a big belly laugh.

CHAPTER 16 - FREQUENT FLYERS

Monkey Man

Every department has them. People who get the police called on them all the time. Trouble just seems to follow them everywhere they go. When I was a police officer in the 1980s and 90's, homeless people were usually not addicted to narcotics like so many are today. Back then, it seems the overwhelming majority of them chose alcohol as their preferred vice. This is the story of six of our most memorable "frequent flyers."

All unique in their own way, they brought out my frustrations and many times my laughter every time I would encounter them. And those encounters were frequent! I mean REALLY frequent!

For example, I can personally remember arresting Lonnie Beal AKA "Monkey Man," no less than 10 times myself. ("Monkey Man" was a nickname he had given to himself). I know other officers from my department had the pleasure of arresting Lonnie many times as well. He was probably the most popular of this august group of individuals.

Lonnie, a black male, was a shorter gentleman (and I use the word "gentleman" loosely). He only stood about 5'4" tall. He loved his alcohol and did outlandish things that got the law called on him many, many, many times.

But his biggest claim to fame, what he was known best for, was that in the jingle jangle department, he was a legend! It dang near hung down to his ankle! He would frequently whip it out and shake it at anyone who happened to be in his vicinity. If he had been entrepreneurial minded, he could have sat by the side of the road and rented himself out as a speed bump or perhaps a parking garage gate! It was enormous and he was proud of it - and rightly so!

The first time I ever saw what nature blessed him with was in the holding cell area of our jail. I had arrested him for something, I can't remember what it was that particular time, and I was in the squad room doing paperwork. I decided I should take a break and look in on my prisoner just to make sure he was ok. When I rounded the corner, Lonnie was in his cell, naked from the waist down, had a two-handed grip on his manhood, and was spinning it around and around like a prop on an airplane.

I was stunned at the mere length of it and questioned myself why I had not noticed it when I patted him down for weapons – both that time and all the other times I had arrested him in the past. I knew no one would believe me if I merely told them what I had seen. I had to find another witness to corroborate my story.

I quickly walked down the hall to the front of the PD in search of someone to show this wonder of science to and since it was midnight shift, most of the building was empty. The first person I found was my sergeant. Sgt. Kathy Mannet. I hesitated only briefly because she was a woman, but I really needed someone - anyone else to see what I had seen!

I said, "Kathy, you have GOT to come back to the holding cell and look at "Monkey Man!" "What's wrong with him?" she said. "Nothing's wrong, you've just got to see this for yourself!" We walked back through the building to the holding cell room and Monkey Man had sat down on his bunk. I said, "Hey Monkey Man, show the Sgt. What you just showed me." Still naked from the waist down, he grinned, sprang to his feet, resumed his two-handed grip, and began spinning it around again.

Now I may be remembering it wrong, but I swear I could feel a breeze coming from his make-shift industrial fan! Meanwhile, Kathy's only response as she marveled at the length of his anaconda was "OH MY GAWD!" When I later told other officers about the experience, I learned that I was late to the party. Many others had also bore witness to what had to be a world record sized pool noodle!

Alvie Miracle

Alvie Miracle, an older white male with a salt and pepper mustache and beard, was the easiest going of all of these fine citizens that I'm describing to you. Sure, he drank like a fish, but he didn't cause too many problems.

Like most of the others, his source of income was panhandling. When I and other officers would respond to calls from citizens about his presence in front of various businesses, he was always apologetic for causing problems and offered to move along. He was never one to argue.

His favorite place to sleep was on a bench in front of the post office. He always had his trusty shopping cart full of his worldly belongings parked by his side. I asked him once why he slept there at night knowing that someone would probably call us on him just for being there. He replied it was a well-lit area and that he was less likely to be harassed by any high school hooligans who might encounter him. Many officers would make him move along just to get him out of public view. But I never did. As far as I was concerned, he wasn't breaking any laws, so I just let him be.

One late night I was patrolling behind businesses looking for burglars or other suspicious activities that might be taking place. As I drove behind an Italian restaurant, some movement caught my eye around the dumpster.

I found Alvie standing in that dumpster, holding a discarded Styrofoam take-out container. He was using his hand as an eating utensil and was slurping up some spaghetti. Sauce was all over his face and beard. I asked him, "Alvie, aren't you afraid of that spaghetti making you sick? You don't have any idea what kind of germs you might be eating!" He looked up at me and replied, "the alcohol will kill the germs." I think he truly believed that was true. Heck, maybe it was! I always thought that his last name couldn't have been more perfect. "MIRACLE." Because as pickled as he always was, it was a miracle that he was alive!

Sarah McClellan

Then, there's Sarah McClellan. What can I say about Sarah? She was a piece of work, let me tell ya! Sarah was a white female, probably in her 50's. Her face was weathered and she looked like she had lived a hard life. She tootled around town on a three wheeled bicycle with her poor hapless Dachshund dog, "Peaches" in the bike's basket which was situated right behind Sarah's butt. Poor dog.

When I would arrest her, as a courtesy, I always took her bike and Peaches back to her house for her. Sarah was retired U.S. Navy. She had a penchant for alcohol like all the others which oftentimes would result in her becoming so intoxicated that she would urinate on herself. I can remember once after arresting her, I took my patrol car to a Do-it-yourself car wash and sprayed the floorboard and back seat out to rid it from the smell of Sarah pee.

What set Sarah apart from all the other frequent flyers, was her ability to string together a VERY, VERY lengthy monologue of curse words when she was mad at you for arresting her. Her cussing skills were actually quite impressive! I always surmised that she developed the art of cussing during her stint in the Navy. She had the foulest mouth I had ever heard from a woman – or a man for that matter!

Because of her time in the military, she got a monthly government check and managed to actually live in a run-down house unlike the other members of this group who for the most part slept out under the stars.

Sarah would occasionally entertain other street people at her humble abode. Other than her government check, she picked up extra money and sometimes liquor from some of the other homeless winos in town by giving them some "special alone time" with her at her ramshackle house. I still cringe merely thinking about that scenario and what must have transpired during that "alone time." Ugh!

William Pitts

William Pitts like Monkey man, was a black male and was small in stature, but to my knowledge wasn't as well endowed. William LOVED his liquor. He usually carried around a plastic cup from a convenience store with his alcohol in it. I guess he figured nobody would ever suspect he had alcohol in the cup instead of a soft drink. Did he really think we were that stupid!?

William always wore long pants and a blue sportscoat in order to look like an upstanding member of society. I don't think the pants were ever washed or the jacket was ever cleaned. Keep in mind this is Florida where the average summer temperature is 90-plus degrees. He still wore that blazer year-round! One whiff of his body odor and alcohol laden breath though, would knock you over.

I'm sure you've heard the expression, "when you've gotta go, you've gotta go." William took that saying to heart and one day, decided to drop his pants while on the edge of the road and take a crap. A car came along and hit William in mid poop! The car fled the scene. The driver to my knowledge was never caught.

Feces was not only down his legs, but smeared eight to ten feet down the road. When police and medics arrived, he was still lying in the road with his pants down around his ankles with pretty substantial injuries. He was transported by ambulance to the hospital and eventually made a full recovery.

William frequently took it upon himself to walk and dance down the middle of the street unofficially leading Christmas parades, MLK parades, and other events held in town – carrying his plastic cup and wearing his sports coat all the while. What got him arrested the most though was his aggressive panhandling technique. He would be very verbally abusive to people who wouldn't give him a buck or two.

Ironically, a number of years later, he was killed in another pedestrian vs. vehicle hit-and-run accident. Not sure if the driver in this hit-and-run was ever caught either. You'll never guess what he was doing when he was hit by a car for a second time. If you guessed taking a crap on the edge of the roadway, you would be correct! William was apparently a very slow learner.

Doris & Billy Ray Tanner

Doris and Billy Ray, a homeless white couple were at the center of many of the complaints we received on street people. Doris and Billy Ray have the distinction of being the only married couple in this group of fine upstanding citizens I'm introducing you to. The antics of these two often made me laugh.

Alcohol played a major role in Doris and Billy Ray's marriage. It would often times lead to spousal arguments in public places. We would have to respond and play referee. The problem was usually resolved by one of them sleeping in another location for the night. Once they sobered up the next day, everything was Mad Dog 20/20 and sunshine again.

Although spousal arguments got the police called on them most frequently, I once responded to a call at a convenience store because Billy Ray had decided to become a community activist.

Apparently, Billy Ray had made a transaction at the store and was upset because he thought he was being over charged. They threw him out of the store but he returned to the public sidewalk a few hours later with a home-made picket sign that had a hand-written message on it that said, "GO HOME FURINERS." An obvious reference to the convenience store owner's country of origin.

I laughed out loud at Billy Ray – to his face - at his atrocious misspelling of the word "foreigners." When I mentioned that his sign was a little difficult to understand, he turned the sign around, looked at it and said, "I don't see anything wrong with it!"

Doris and Billy Ray's main residence was underneath an abandoned citrus semi-trailer. I was surprised one night to be dispatched to a disturbance call at some run-down apartments near the high school and was told to make contact with the complainant, Doris Tanner. I was confused. They were street people and the dispatcher was sending me to an actual apartment building to see Doris.

When I arrived, Doris was the only one there and was in good spirits. Her and Billy Ray had argued earlier but he had left already. With a big grin on her face, Doris took me by the arm and proceeded to give me the grand tour of their apartment. I could tell she was so proud to be living in an actual apartment albeit a run-down, low-rent building.

I obliged her and she showed me the sparsely furnished living room and a mattress on the floor of the bedroom that served as their bed. When we got to the kitchen, Doris turned on the water faucet to show me that they had running water. She was so proud of her new home! To her, it might as well have been a multimillion-dollar mansion.

I told Doris that I was happy for her but I had other calls I need to go to. Still holding onto my arm, she said, "let me show you something else." She led me to the bathroom and showed me the toilet flush. She just went on and on about it.

I listened patiently for a while, but needed to get back in service. Still chit-chatting about her apartment's amenities, I finally interrupted her and jokingly asked her, "Doris, did you call me here for a real problem or just to look at my pretty face? She bowed her head slightly, smiled a partially toothless grin, batted her eyes and said, "Just to look at your pretty face." She was a hoot!

There were others similar to these frequent flyers that my fellow officers and I dealt with on a regular basis, but these six... These six made a lasting impression on me and I'm sure on my co-workers as well.

They're all gone now. May they all rest in peace at that big distillery in the sky.

Chapter 17 – A ONE-MAN SWAT TEAM & THE APPLIANCE STORE BURGLAR

One for the road

I got a call about a drunk passed out in the middle of the road. I had received other calls like this. A lot of times, a drunk driver would stop at a traffic light and decide that it was time for a little nap. That wasn't the case this time.

When I arrived, there was no car anywhere in sight. There was however a heavyset white guy lying on his back, stretched out across the center line of the roadway. My Sgt. at the time, Kathy Mannet who you'll remember from the "Monkey Man" story, drove by to back me up. The guy was so drunk, he couldn't even form a sentence. Kathy and I mutually decided it would be a good idea to remove the guy from the roadway for his safety and ours.

We tried to roust him awake to no avail. We were able to get his wallet out of his back pocket so we could I.D. him though. Too drunk to walk on his own accord, we grabbed his arms and dragged him to the side of the road and leaned him against a telephone pole while I conducted a warrants check.

As we were waiting for dispatch to come back with the warrants check, we soon noticed the guy making unusual movements like he was swatting at imaginary flies. We noticed that he seemed to be directing his swats more toward himself and around his lower back and butt crack area that had become a bit more exposed during the dragging process.

A bit later, the warrants check came back negative and we decided to take him down to our holding cell and let him continue to sleep it off there. We realized while trying to get him to his feet again to put him in the patrol car that where we had leaned him up against the telephone pole, there was a large fire ant bed.

Ants had devoured the back side of his "southern region." As far as I know, the PD was never billed for anti-itch cream for his butt crack.

Freeze! Don't move!

At the Sheriff's Office I had a take-home patrol car. But, at the Winter Haven Police Department, officers shared cars. At shift change, the parking lot was a beehive of activity as one officer removed his gear and the officer coming on duty loaded his stuff into the car. One thing that wasn't transferred during this process was the flashlight. The flashlight was a rechargeable light that slid into a mounted charging cradle so that it was always ready when an officer needed to light the darkness.

On this particular night, it was raining during the move-in/move out procedure. So, both I and the other officer who was getting off duty were moving our stuff quickly. I noticed when I was putting my things into the patrol car that the flashlight was lying on the front seat instead of being in the charging cradle. I wondered how long it had been off the charger during his shift. I stuck it in the charger and didn't think anything more about it.

I answered a few calls and each time I used the flashlight, I noticed that it was only good for about five minutes or so and then it would just go from bright to dim to not even working at all. Leaving it off the charger the previous shift shouldn't have made it perform like this. I wondered if the cell had gone bad and if the officer who used the patrol car on the previous shift had left it on the seat to remind himself to tell me that it was malfunctioning. Perhaps he had forgotten to do so because of our rushing around in the rain to move our gear in and out at shift change.

It was a busy night for calls. Every time it would rain, false burglar alarms would be triggered at businesses all over the city. It was pretty common. Even though it was raining, we were obligated to check out each and every alarm as if it were the real thing.

About two in the morning, I was dispatched to an appliance store for – you guessed it – a burglar alarm. As I pulled into the front lot, I could see that the glass doors and windows in the front were all intact. So far, so good. I grabbed the flashlight and got out of my patrol car wearing my oh-so fashionable yellow raincoat, and started checking the loading bay and back door of the business.

The bay door was secure, but when I tried the regular door, it was unlocked! I reported to dispatch that I had found an open door and was going in to search the business since we had no K-9 units available that night. Everyone else was busy on their own calls so, I was on my own. With flashlight in my left hand and my now drawn .45 caliber 1911 in my right hand, I swung the door open and began my search.

The electricity to the store had been knocked out by the storm. The only light in the store was from the emergency exit lights and my "trusty" flashlight. At this point, I know you're way ahead of me here. Predictably, the flashlight died on me. My eyes slowly began to adjust to the dimly lit store's interior. There were still areas in the store that were pitch black. It was a dangerous situation to say the least. I pushed forward. Relying on my hearing as much as my eyesight, I cautiously searched the storeroom and moved on into the showroom.

The showroom was a little easier to see in - although it was still very dimly lit. There were a lot of washing machines and dryers that someone could hide behind. It was a bit nerve racking. Everything checked out ok until I got about to the mid-way point in the store. There was suddenly a flash of lightning that momentarily lit up part of the store up near the plate glass windows. It was during that lightning flash that I saw the silhouette of the burglar!

Aiming the business end of my semi-auto at his torso, I began shouting at him to, "GET ON THE FLOOR! GET ON THE FLOOR!" He ignored my orders and just stood there frozen from what I assumed was sheer terror at being caught red-handed by the police.

Several more authoritative shouts from me went ignored. As I inched closer, ready to dive behind a nearby washing machine if he raised a gun at me, another flash of lightening streaked across the sky outside illuminating the store's interior once again.

It was at this moment that I was glad I didn't have back-up on this call to witness what I had done. I had been screaming and shouting orders to a cardboard standee of an appliance repairman. I laughed at myself a bit and was relieved that number 1, there were no burglars in the store and number 2, I didn't have to explain to my supervisors and the store managers why I shot a hole through their cardboard standee and the front plate glass window! Whew! An even bigger embarrassment than yelling at an inanimate object avoided!

As for the open door where I came in – it simply had been unintentionally left unlocked by an employee when they closed up the night before.

CHAPTER 18 - HITCHING A RIDE

<u>**Scott**</u>

During my employment at WHPD, I continued to moonlight as a professional magician. It was difficult to schedule shows because of a monthly rotating shift schedule. One month I would be on day shift, the next on midnight shift, and the next on evening shift. My days off also changed from month to month and I was also subject to call-out if something major went down. Normally, if I had a big, well-paying show coming up, I would put in well in advance for the day/night off. Whether I would get that day or night off was always a little iffy. But I made it work.

For a number of years, I performed at the police department's employee Christmas party. It was a lot of fun showing my peers another side of me they had never seen before. The Chief of the police department himself even once hired me to perform close-up magic for a luncheon he hosted for other police chiefs in the area.

Of course being just as involved in magic as I was police work, my friendship with other magicians continued to strengthen. Curious about my role as a police officer, a few of my friends expressed an interest in doing an officer ride-along with me during one of my shifts.

One of my friends was the young man I mentioned earlier in this book named Scott Huston. I went through the proper channels and made the official requests for Scott, then 18 or 19 years old, to do his ride-along with me. A background check was conducted on him and a date was set.

As we patrolled the city, many of our conversations were about performing and specific magic tricks. We went on a couple theft calls, a loud noise complaint, and a few other incidents that were rather routine and mundane to me, but to Scott, it was like being in a real-life police movie.

As part of the pre-ride-along briefing, Scott was told to remain in the car on any hot calls we might be dispatched to until we cleared the scene and it was safe. He had NO PROBLEM with that! He was there to see action, not be involved in it.

I happened to be on midnight shift when Scott was riding with me. I was well accustomed to the hours, but Scott was up way past his normal time of going to bed. I noticed around three o'clock or so his eyes were getting heavy and our conversations had slowed. I said, "you look pretty tired man, do you want me to take you back to the PD so you can get your car and go home?" He said, "No, I'm ok. I don't want to miss anything."

A little while later, I got one of those hot calls we had talked about before the ride-along. It was a burglar alarm. We sped across town, blue lights flashing and at a high rate of speed to get there. The adrenaline was pumping through Scott. When in his life would he ever get to legally speed and violate traffic signal lights or witness up close an exciting police call like this?

The other officer responding as back-up and I arrived about the same time. It was a shopping village type area on the south-west side of town with a number of different businesses. Scott remained in the car while the other officer and I began checking out the businesses. There were several shops so it probably took us about ten minutes to check every door and window. Everything was secure. It was a false alarm.

As we started walking back to our cars, I saw Scott's head against the window. He was fast asleep. I guess getting there was exciting, but waiting for us to return to the car was boring. Being so tired, he had just conked out. The other officer and I laughed about it and I said, "watch this!" I walked up to the passenger side of the car and banged repeatedly on the glass while screaming. Scott jolted awake!

At first, he wasn't sure where he was. He looked out the front windshield and saw nothing. Then, he looked over and saw my face up against the glass, with my flashlight pointing up from my chin, illuminating my face in a spooky manner. He jumped in fright a second time! I just love messing with people!

After we cleared that call, Scott decided that he should probably go home. Even though he was having so much fun, he was just too tired to continue any longer.

Tommy

The second magician buddy of mine to do a ride-along with me was Tommy Jason. Tommy rode with me on evening shift. I don't remember it being a very busy night so Tommy and I had a lot of time to chat about magic and about a card trick in particular. As I mentioned earlier, there isn't much about card magic that Tommy doesn't know.

As he was explaining this one particular trick to me, I was dispatched to a shoplifter call. I was less than a block away from the convenience store where the shoplifting had occurred. I told Tommy, "Let's pause this conversation until after this call." He agreed.

Tommy waited in the car while I went inside to talk to the clerk. I learned from the clerk that the suspect was still on the property! He was sitting on the sidewalk in front of the store. I got the information I needed from the clerk and at the same time, kept an eye on the suspect in case he decided to stand up and leave. After I finished with the clerk, I went outside to arrest the suspect. He was drunk and belligerent. He pulled away from me a little, but wasn't really fighting me. I got him handcuffed and put him into the back seat of the patrol car.

When I sat back down in the driver's seat, I performed a wanted persons check on the guy. While I'm waiting for it to come back, Tommy started explaining the card trick again to me. "You put the aces on top of the deck and put five indifferent cards on top of the aces. And then…"

The focus of our conversation was shattered by the sound of the handcuffed suspect shouting profanities and actively trying to kick out the window of the patrol car. He had suddenly become an angry drunk.

I told Tommy, "Hang on a second." I got out of the car, opened the rear door and snatched the prisoner out of the unit. I threw him hard over the trunk of the car and in my "cop voice" told him in no uncertain terms to stop kicking my window. I may have uttered some angry expletives as well.

After my cop/suspect conversation with him, I put him back in the back of the patrol car and got back into the driver's seat. Without looking up, I calmly asked Tommy, "ok, so how many indifferent cards are on top of the aces?"

Tommy didn't immediately reply, so I casually looked over at him. His back was pressed against his passenger side door and he was staring at me, mouth agape, with a hint of fear in his eyes. He only knew me as mild-mannered Dale the magician. He had never seen me flip the switch from easy going friendly guy into angry, authoritative police officer mode before.

I think it stunned him and he was a little bit afraid of me there for a few seconds. He recovered relatively quickly but I heard a slight quiver in his voice as he finished explaining the card trick to me that we had been talking about.

He has never forgotten about that experience and still occasionally mentions my ability to transform from Dr. Jekyll to Mr. Hyde and then back to Dr. Jekyll so quickly and effortlessly.

Doug

My magician buddy, Doug Anders never got the opportunity to do a citizen orientation ride-along with me. But once when my wife and I were driving him to the port in Tampa to join a ship as a guest entertainer, a funny thing happened. Well, it was funny to me anyway.

The Port of Tampa is not situated in the best of areas. There are strip clubs, hookers, and drug dealers all over the area. Doug, even though he had been in that area to join ships many times before, was still wary of the criminal element that inhabited the area.

We were having a conversation about drug dealers approaching the car. I told him about my experience working under-cover narcotics and told him, "There's nothing to be scared of. Generally, they won't approach a car unless you give them the international, I want to buy drugs sign."

He asked, "what's the sign?" I said, here, "I'll show you." I reached back and took out my wallet. I removed a twenty-dollar bill and folded it lengthwise one time. At the next traffic signal, I saw a young man who looked to me like he was probably an illegal pharmaceutical salesman sitting about twenty feet from the roadway on a milk crate. I waved the bill at him as I held it between my index and middle fingers.

He got up from his seated position and started walking toward my driver's window. Just then, the light turned green and Doug said anxiously, "DRIVE, DRIVE, DRIVE!" He was relieved to be out of his perceived danger.

He didn't know at the time that driving away before the drug dealer got to the car was my intention all along. I never rolled my window down and had subtly timed the light so I would have a green signal when I waved the bill at him. Plus, I had my .38 snub-nosed pistol in my ankle holster in case anything would have gone south.

Lynn and I dropped Doug off at the port and chuckled about his response on our way home. I had never seen him rattled like that before and it still makes us smile thinking about it even now. And as for Doug... Yep, he still remembers that incident from thirty years ago. It apparently made a long-lasting memory for him. If my antics are nothing else, they're memorable.

CHAPTER 19 - POLICE PRANKS

Porkchop

I'm about to tell you about a LOT of pranks I pulled, other officers pulled, and one in the next chapter that was pulled on me. Reading about all these, one might get the impression that all police officers do is play around while at work. Nothing could be further from the truth. We spend the largest majority of our time answering calls for service and writing reports.

Some of the rotting bodies, blood, brains, guts, abused animals, brutal injuries, suicides, murders, abused children, and other tragedies we see would turn most people's stomach. There were sights that can never be unseen. Smells that linger in our minds for decades. Sounds of cries from mothers who just lost their child that ring in our heads well after retirement. Is it any wonder that we pull pranks on our co-workers to give us a momentary smile and relieve a little stress every once in a while?

The earliest police prank award by a Garrett has to go to my brother, Gary. When he first started his career in law enforcement in 1971, walkie talkie radios were pretty uncommon. I mean they existed, but most people had never seen one.

During that time period, Gary was a patrolman in the small city of Frostproof, Florida. Just like in Mayberry, the town of Frostproof had their town drunk. When I interviewed him for this book, my brother couldn't remember the guy's real name, but his nickname was "Porkchop." Porkchop would stumble down the street almost every weekend on his way home from the one and only bar in town.

Gary knew where he lived and knew the route he always took going home. One Saturday night, he saw Porkchop making his weekly trek from the bar to his house. Gary drove on ahead of him and rounded a corner where he noticed a city trashcan on the sidewalk. That's when the idea hit him. He hid a walkie talkie in the trash can underneath discarded papers and assorted trash. He parked across the street under a tree in the shadows and waited for Porkchop's arrival.

Right on cue, Porkchop rounded the corner and as soon as he got even with the trashcan, my brother spoke to him through the walkie talkie. "Hey Porkchop!" said Gary. Porkchop stopped, looked around and didn't see anyone.

He started to continue walking when my brother spoke to him again. "Hey Porkchop, where you going?" The town was small, there was no traffic and the night was still, so Gary could easily hear Porkchops response because not only was he a town drunk, he was a loud talker as well. "Who just said that?" asked Porkchop. Gary responded, "it's me, the trashcan!" "Well how the heck are ya?" slurred Porkchop. Gary replied, "I'm good. Just hanging around collecting people's trash. How are you doing?"

Porkchop leaned against the wall of the building to support himself and replied, "I'm drunker than I've ever been!" Gary responded, "well, just how drunk are you Porkchop?" Porkchop paused for a moment as if in deep contemplation of the question and replied, "I'm so drunk, I'm talking to a trashcan!"

It was all Gary could do to not laugh too loud and give away his hiding spot across the street. "Well, I've gotta go home now." said Porkchop. "OK, have a good one buddy" Gary said. Porkchop stumbled on toward his house. He made it about fifteen feet and turned around and shouted, "Goodnight, Mr. Trashcan!" Gary lost it!

Who's messing with Lieutenant Dan?

At WHPD, there was a Lieutenant named Dan Elette. Dan had a brilliant mind! He knew the law like the back of his hand. He could cite from memory exact statute numbers of laws. Everyone else had to look them up. And not only did he know all the common laws that were frequently broken, he knew all the obscure laws and city ordinances as well.

If Dan had one character flaw, it was paranoia. He was somewhat of a conspiracy theorist and was always on guard against the chief and higher-ranking members of the administration spying on him.

My brother Carl got a birthday card one year for his birthday. It was one of those electronic birthday cards that played a little tune whenever someone opened the card. Eventually the battery died on it and Carl ripped it open, curious to see the mechanism that produced the music. The mechanism was a tiny computer circuit board with a small flat speaker attached to it to play the music. The gears in Carl's head started to spin.

He removed the device from the card and taped it under Lieutenant Dan's desk but he left one of the tiny wires slightly sticking out just a little so it would be noticed. It didn't take long. Dan came stomping out of his office with the mock listening device in hand, complaining to everyone he encountered, "SEE! I knew the east end was spying on me!" He promptly took it out to the sally-port and crushed the gadget with the heel of his boot. I don't think Carl ever told him it was just a joke.

Elette in addition to being a fountain of knowledge when it came to the law was also feared by rookies because he was a stickler for rules and department policies.

My brother Gary came in to possession of a rubber snake that looked hyper realistic. He coiled it up and put it under Lieutenant Dan's office desk. His reaction was predictable. He jumped up and screamed! Gary came back in laughing at him. Elette and Gary had a good working relationship and Dan jokingly told Gary if he ever did something like that again, he would shoot him!

A couple of the rookie officers who feared Lieutenant Dan later told Gary they couldn't believe he did that to Elette of all people. Gary just chuckled at them, shrugged, and said, "he's just a man like all of us." Gary and Dan developed a close friendship. Even after both of them retired and Gary had moved to Tennessee, they would speak to each other on the phone weekly until Dan's untimely death. He was an interesting man.

Green with envy

I don't know where he obtained it, but my brother Carl came into possession of a small container of Visible Theft Detection Powder. Visible stain theft detection powder is used to trap thieves by applying to objects likely to be stolen. Think dye-packs used in banks. This stuff was amazing! If you got any on your skin, even a small amount, it would stain your skin green. Of course, he didn't have it long when his thoughts turned from using it as a theft deterrent tool to using it as a practical joke.

An officer named Chuck Heikes was a bit gruff and distant when it came to associating with his fellow officers. He was always serious and didn't really joke around like the rest of the officers. I'm not sure why Carl chose him as his victim, but he did.

Carl got to work early and went into the locker room. Chuck stored his uniform hat on top of his locker. Carl carefully sprinkled some of the powder on the inside band of the hat.

Naturally, when Chuck put on the hat, the powder not only made contact with his forehead, but sprinkles of it fell down on the rest of his face. Glancing in the mirror, Chuck immediately recognized that some type of foreign green powdery substance was on his face!

His immediate reaction, like any other rational person, was to try to wash it off in the sink. That was a colossal mistake! The problem was, this stuff didn't wash off. In fact, water only amplified its intensity and caused the green color to spread even more.

Poor Chuck's face looked like a watermelon – green with darker green lines running from his forehead to his chin. He was angry with a capital A! His hands were also green from trying to wash them in the sink. He stormed out of the locker room and into the squad room demanding to know if the maintenance person had been using some sort of new cleaning powder in the locker room.

Everyone tried their best to stifle their laughter. Chuck was furious! In fact, he was so mad about it, Carl never confessed to him that he was the perpetrator of this cruel prank. But I guess if Chuck reads this book, he'll finally know who to blame. Good times.

The Don of a new era

Regardless of what motivated Carl to prank Chuck the way he did, I personally, 99% of the time, would only pull pranks on people I liked. My targets were good natured, had a sense of humor, didn't get mad at me, and still maintained their friendships with me after the prank was over.

So, if my criteria for pulling pranks was to do them to people who I liked, then I must have liked Officer Donnie Bigley a LOT! Donnie was just an easy target and laughed along even though I often targeted him as the victim of my many shenanigans. I loved that guy. Still do!

Like myself, Donnie was a young officer and we worked on the same shift together for a lot of years. Heck, we even went through the police academy together and were in the same graduating class. We spent many days, evenings, and nights working calls together and backing each other up on hot calls. We could always depend on each other.

I cannot begin to recall all the pranks I played on Donnie, but the following three stand out the most in my memory. Ironically, my association with magic is directly responsible for all three.

Donnie had a bad habit. Every time we would meet up on duty and park driver's window to driver's window, he would notice that I was chewing gum and would bum a piece off of me. I was like, "Why can't you go buy your own gum!?" He replied, "why should I do that when I can get it from you for free?"

On my off-duty trips to magic shops, I would often peruse the joke counter looking for ideas. I found the perfect item! It was a pack of joke chewing gum that as you chewed it, would temporarily dye your mouth dark blue. What is it about us Garrett Brothers dying people's skin and mouths!?

The joke gum itself looked somewhat similar to what I normally chewed, but the packaging wasn't even close. To make this work, I was going to need to do some prep-work. I carefully unwrapped the joke gum and rewrapped it in the same foil and paper sleeve as my regular brand. I folded the edge of the corner of the paper sleeve over slightly to distinguish the joke gum from the regular pieces in the pack.

My plan was to meet up with Donnie and be chewing a piece of gum. I knew if I offered him a piece, he would become suspicious and think something was up. So, we met up again driver's side window to driver's side window just to shoot the breeze. Waiting for him to ask me for a piece of gum was agonizing. But I maintained my cool. Eventually, just as I had planned, he said, "hey, give me a piece of gum man." Feigning my frustration about him always bumming gum from me I gave him the trick gum.

When he unwrapped it, he briefly questioned the appearance of the gum. I just blew it off by saying, "all of the pieces look like that now." Donnie shrugged and popped the piece of gum in his mouth. We sat there and chatted for another two or three minutes and I glanced over at him. This joke gum had worked like a champ! Not only was his mouth and tongue dark blue, but his teeth were blue and his lips were blue as well! I tried my hardest to not burst out in laughter, but I knew if I sat there any longer, I was going to explode. I quickly wrapped up our conversation by saying, I needed to go use the bathroom at the PD and we parted company.

I drove as fast as the law allowed directly to the police department. But instead of going to the bathroom, I went and immediately found our Lieutenant, Mary Mariotti. Mary loved to laugh and I knew she was going to get a kick out of my latest stunt. I told her, "You have got to call Donnie and tell him to return to the station!" "OK, why?" she asked. "I gave him some trick gum! Call him in and look at his mouth when he gets here!" She did as I requested.

Mary and I were both standing in the hall next to the dispatcher's window when Donnie checked out on the radio at the PD. My anticipation was at a fever pitch! Donnie walked in and strolled over to where Mary and I were standing and said, "hey what's up?" He could see that we were both smiling, so he smiled as well. When he did, Mary got sight of his blue tinged teeth and just burst out laughing.

She actually doubled over belly-laughing at how ridiculous he looked. Donnie had no clue what we were both now laughing about and he started laughing as well. Mary caught enough of her breath, and wiping away her tears of laughter told Donnie, "Go look in a mirror!" He did and knew immediately exactly how it had happened and who was responsible for it!

Another trip to a magic shop meant another shopping spree for a good practical joke to play on Donnie. I found a little metal device that was called a "Car Exhaust Whistle." The idea was to put it into the tail pipe of someone's car and it would make a whistling noise when it was started.

I caught Donnie out on a routine call and while he was busy, I did the deed. I pushed the silver metal device several inches into his patrol car's tail pipe so he couldn't see it if he just casually looked at it. I parked my own car close by but out of sight. When he cleared the call, he drove past me. To my surprise, and I'm sure to his, it didn't make a whistling noise, it was more of a sound you would hear from a cartoon space ship. It sounded ridiculously funny! I decided to just let him continue to drive around with it on his patrol car for a while instead of telling him immediately what I had done.

Thirty minutes later I was patrolling by the mall. I saw Donnie's patrol car in the parking lot and he was kneeling down looking up the tail pipe with his flash light. I thought to myself, "Oh no, he has discovered the device and is going to put two and two together and know that I was the one responsible."

I pulled over next to him and innocently asked, "what are you doing?" He said, "my car's making a weird noise but I think I've found what's causing it." I exited my own patrol car and walked over to the back of his. He said, "use my flashlight and look in the tail pipe. Is that supposed to be in there?"

I dutifully got down on one knee and peered into his tail pipe with the light. I said, "are you talking about that silver thing in there?" He said yeah, that's it!" I replied, that can't be what's causing it, that's your catalytic converter man!" Exasperated, he scratched his head and said, "well, then I don't know what's causing this noise. But it's damn annoying!"

I guess I felt like the joke had run its course at this point so I let him in on the gag. He jokingly called me a few expletives and we used a coat hanger to remove the whistling device. It was probably reusable, but I recall tossing it into a nearby dumpster. It had served its purpose and had been money well-spent.

Yet another trip to the magic shop meant another great find at the practical joke counter. Donnie was excited about his upcoming vacation. He had nine long relaxing days coming up to rest and relax from the stressors of the job and my relentless practical joke shenanigans.

Something else Donnie was excited about at that time was the lottery. The state of Florida had just a few months before, legalized lottery tickets in the state. Donnie was convinced that one day soon, he was going to hit it big and retire from the department a millionaire. Recognizing his enthusiasm for the lottery I plotted this practical joke.

Home computers weren't very prevalent back then much less home printers. As I recall, printer technology was still pretty much in the "dot matrix" stage of development at the time.

At the joke counter at the magic shop, they had a number of very professionally designed and printed brightly colored envelopes with things printed on them such as "pregnancy test results enclosed" and "gay cruise confirmation details inside!" The one that caught my eye said, "Congratulation lottery winner, payout details enclosed!" Perfect!

I scratched out a little short poem on a piece of paper that read, "Roses are red, violets are blue. Even if you're on vacation, I can still get you!" I waited until Donnie's first day of vacation and popped it in the mail to him. I knew I wasn't going to be there for the joke, but thought it'll give him a little chuckle while he's on vacation.

When he came back from vacation, I asked him before briefing started if he got excited when he received the envelope in the mail. He then went on to relate how I got him this time even better than I had planned.

He said that he was in Orlando, about an hour from Winter Haven. He was there to meet with his ex-wife and spend a couple days with his son. His mother phoned him at his ex-wife's home and told him, "Donnie, you got something from the lottery commission. It looks important! It says you're a lottery winner on the envelope! Do you want me to open it?" Donnie replied, "NO! ABSOLUTELY NOT! I'll be right home!"

He left right in the middle of his visit and admitted that he sped down Interstate 4 to get home to get his hands on this good news! He was so sure that he was Florida's newest lottery winner that he said he wasn't even worried about getting a speeding ticket because he would now have plenty of money to pay the fine.

When he got home, his car had barely rolled to a stop in his driveway before he bolted out of it and sprinted into the house. He was immediately reminded that I was a practical joke master and a half-assed poet at best. Talk about getting the air let out of your sails.

He took it in stride as he did all of my shenanigans. To Donnie (or Don as you now prefer to be called), thanks for being a good sport. Thanks for not shooting me for the constant barrage of practical jokes I pulled on you. But most of all, thanks for being a life-long friend.

My prank masterpiece: Charlie Burke's big adventure

Some pranks require very little set-up or preparation. This one was just the opposite. It took a lot of pre-planning, involved multiple co-conspirators, and had a lot of moving parts. I'm proud to say it was solely my own brainchild.

A new rookie officer named Charlie Burke came to our squad. A bit younger than me by a few years, Charlie was an excitable individual. Once I backed him up on a loud music noise complaint at a lake-side bar. He had previously given multiple warnings to the bar owner about keeping the noise levels down.

On this particular call, he got angry at the bar owner and began yelling at him. You could see the veins in Charlie's forehead and neck beginning to show. When he got chest to chest with the guy, I thought he needed to cool down the situation a bit. I mean after all; it was just a noise complaint.

I didn't say a word, but standing quietly behind him, I reached down and grabbed the back of his gun belt and slowly pulled him backward – like you would a dog leash if your dog was about to get into a fight with another dog. It worked and we peacefully resolved the issue without anyone getting into a fight or going to jail.

What makes a practical joke work the best is when the prank centers around the intended victim's weaknesses. I recognized Charlie's excitability as his Achilles heel, and that's when I began to think of a plan of attack.

Charlie arrested a guy for something. It may have been

shoplifting or some other minor offense. The guy gave Charlie a fake name and Charlie released him on a notice to appear in court rather than taking him to jail.

Charlie later found out from another officer what the guy's real name was and that he had a lengthy criminal history and outstanding warrants. This made Charlie MAD! He wanted revenge on this guy who had dared to lie to a law enforcement officer! As I said, Charlie was new and hadn't yet learned that criminals lie to cops on a regular basis.

On the warpath to arrest this guy, Charlie spent two nights trying to locate him at previous known addresses, friends and relative's addresses, and area motels and hotels. The guy he was looking for was somewhat nomadic, part time homeless, and didn't stay in any one place very long.

My plan was to make Charlie's anger at the guy to be the engine that drove my prank. I assembled my team of co-conspirators made up of three other guys on my shift; Rick Heinlin, Byran Combles, and Jim Johnson.

Rick's job was to call Charlie on the radio and have him meet up with him in the parking lot of a camping supply store. Once Charlie arrived, Rick was to lure Charlie away from his car by telling him that an informant had told Rick that the guy Charlie had been looking for was sleeping in an alley just across the street from the camping store.

Byran, who was off duty that night like I was, had a critical role. After Rick lured Charlie out of direct sight of his patrol car, his job was to take the extra patrol car key that I had surreptitiously obtained at the police department, open Charlie's driver's side door, and roll the electric window all the way down.

Then, Byran was to pour a container of broken auto glass that I had obtained from a local wrecker service, on Charlie's front seat and on the parking lot next to his car's door. Then, he was to put a big gnarly rock, about the size of a grapefruit that I had obtained on Charlie's front driver's seat. Lastly, Byran was to take a pillowcase full of Mason jars and smash them on the ground. The thought was that Charlie would be able to hear this in the still of the night, even though he was in the alley across the street and was some distance away.

Jim's job was to call Charlie on the radio and tell him to switch over off the main channel. Once there, Jim was to inform Charlie that someone had flagged him down and told him that he saw the guy Charlie was looking for messing around his unattended patrol car at the camping supply store. He also was to tell him that he would be in the area attempting to locate him. Lastly, Jim's job was to pick up Byran at a predetermined location after Byran had smashed the Mason jars and bolted from the scene.

My job? Besides orchestrating this symphony of shenanigans was to video tape and narrate the whole thing from my vehicle parked in the tire repair business right next door to the camping store.

At exactly 2:00 AM on the night of the prank, the whole thing played out almost exactly as I have described above. The only thing that didn't work out was the smashing of the jars in the pillowcase. Neither Rick or Charlie heard the glass breaking. I had to do something to let Rick know that the scene had been set and to guide Charlie back to their patrol cars. I clicked the mic on my radio several times and Rick picked up on the clue.

Meanwhile, Jim interpreted those radio clicks to mean that he was to tell Charlie about the guy he was looking for messing around the patrol cars at the camping store. In just a few moments, Charlie came hard charging from the alley across the street followed by Rick.

When Charlie got to his car, he was shining his flashlight into his front seat on the rock and broken glass. Byran had added an additional touch and took one of the larger intact pieces of auto glass and wedged it into the rubber window sill to further the illusion that the window had been smashed out. Charlie was livid! He was veins protruding from his forehead and neck again livid!

After about one minute of letting him build up even more steam, Jim called Charlie on the citizen band radio we all were running in our patrol cars at the time, and told Charlie, "I got him! It's the guy you've been looking for! He's 10-15!" (In custody). Charlie replied on the CB radio, "bring his butt back here!"

While waiting for Jim to arrive with his "prisoner," another officer, Sarah Johnson, who wasn't in on the joke drove by in her patrol car and stopped at the edge of the parking lot. Charlie shouted to her "that mother***** busted out my window!" Rick walked over to her car and quietly told her, "Ignore everything. It's a practical joke in progress." She just shook her head and drove away.

About that same time, Jim pulled into the parking lot with Byran in the back seat wearing a hoodie and concealing his face. Charlie started stomping over to Jim's unit but before he could get there, Jim jumped out and opened the back door. Byran jumped out of the car laughing. Rick was laughing, Jim was laughing, and I, still hidden while filming and narrating the video, was laughing. Charlie was just dumbfounded and confused. He realized that he had been the victim of a joke.

When things calmed down a bit, Charlie said, "you guys sure go a long way for a joke busting my window out like that!" He still thought his window was broken! Laughter all around again as Rick sat down in Charlies unit, put the key in the ignition, and rolled the window up – revealing the gag.

I remained hidden the entire time. Charlie never knew I was there. At least not until the next day at briefing. I got our lieutenant in on it and brought her up to speed on what we had done. Lieutenant Mary Mariotti finished briefing and announced that we had been ordered by the brass to watch this training video. She popped the VHS cassette into the player and we all got to laugh at poor Charlie all over again while he tried to conceal the fact that his face was crimson red from embarrassment.

After I retired from the department, Charlie remained and continued to rise in the ranks. Eventually, he was promoted to the position of Chief of Police! I like to think I played a small part in his formative years as a young police officer on handling situations without blinding yourself with rage.

In fact, he stated to me just a few years ago during a phone conversation that he thanks me for those lessons in humility, anger management, and being humble. He said they served him well during the rest of his career and in his position as Chief.

CHAPTER 20 - THE PRANKSTER GETS PRANKED

Through the years, I have orchestrated many pranks on many of my fellow officers. Some were small pranks, and some, like the one with Charlie Burke were very elaborate.

Some of the officers who I pranked thought they would retaliate against me and play a prank on me. They rarely worked as planned.

One example was when an officer set up a Styrofoam cup of water on top of my locker and attached a fishing line from the top of the cup to my locker door in an effort to have the water pour on my head when I opened the locker door. The white Styrofoam cup stuck out like a sore thumb and I noticed it immediately on top of my locker when I walked into the room. His set-up was discovered and quickly diffused. It failed.

When people attempted to prank me, I would either figure out what was going on before it happened or the joke itself was ill-conceived or just a lame prank.

There was one glaring exception to that. But it wasn't an officer from my own squad who pulled it off. I was "prank victimized" by my closest rivals in the practical joke business. The attack came from much closer to home. My own brothers! After all, they were raised by the same father I was. Shenanigans are in my family's DNA.

To make a little extra money, I signed up to take an off-duty detail. It was easy work. It was basically a stakeout on a retail store that was remodeling. They had to remove all of the front plate glass windows of the store during the remodeling process. They had tacked up some plywood to deter burglars from entering the department store and removing whatever they pleased.

As an extra layer of security, they hired a police officer to sit in front of the store in a marked police car during the overnight hours. I didn't park right in front of the building though. I was almost the entire parking lot away - but had a clear view of the entire front of the store. My intent wasn't to deter a burglar, but to try to catch one red-handed.

Watching the front of a business all night is a boring job. So, about midnight, I was happy to see my brothers, Gary and Carl pull up in their personal vehicle to chat and keep me company for a bit. We sat there chatting and shooting the breeze for probably thirty minutes when I looked over at the front of the store and saw movement.

A shabbily dressed wino in a hoodie stumbled up the sidewalk in front of the store, pausing a few times to lean against the wall. I thought to myself, "Oh man, this guy is double D drunk!"

Eventually, the drunk stopped in front of the store and started pulling at the plywood trying to gain entry into the building. I intently watched and waited. One of my brother's spoke up and said, "Aren't you going to go check him out?" I said, "No. I don't have a good charge yet. If he gets the plywood off and tries to enter, I've got a burglary collar!"

I waited and watched some more. The wino started stumbling away from the building. I told my brothers, "He's not going to get in, but at least I've got him for loitering and prowling."

As I sped across the parking lot in the patrol car, I heard the most terrible metallic noise I've ever heard dragging under my patrol car. I was focused on the "criminal" and some part of my brain told me, "Oh crap! Your gas tank just fell off and is being dragged under the car!" But the car was still going so I continued to focus on the wino who by now had rounded the corner and was walking down the side of the building.

I caught up to him, jumped out of my car and shouted, "HEY YOU, STOP!" Instead of stopping, he kept on walking at an even quicker pace! I jumped back in my patrol car and sped closer to him. The gas tank still scraping the parking lot! I jumped out of my car again and gave chase! Just about the time I caught up to him, my brothers came around the corner in their car - I thought to back me up.

Suddenly, just about the time I caught up to the wino and started to put my hands on him, he spun around and pulled his hoodie backward revealing his face, or should I say, HER face!? It was Gary's wife, Lindy! Lindy, also a sworn officer played a very convincing wino. I had been totally fooled! Meanwhile Carl and Gary said they came around the corner to where we were as quickly as they did to stop me from potentially shooting Lindy or taking her down hard.

We all laughed for a bit and I suddenly remembered that during all the excitement when I was pursuing Lindy and driving across the parking lot, my gas tank had fallen off. I told them about it at the same time I was walking to the back of my patrol car to check out the damage. Instead, what I found was a large two foot by three-foot piece of sheet metal attached to the back of my car with a chain!

During the time Gary and I were chatting, he was really distracting me while Carl secretly attached the piece of sheet metal to my car. It was very well done. I didn't catch them or suspect a thing.

Gary asked me, "If you thought your gas tank had fallen off, how did you think the patrol car was still able to be driven?" I replied, "I don't know, I'm not a mechanic! But I figured as long as I pushed the gas pedal and the car was still moving forward, I was going to keep speeding toward the suspect. I was focused and determined to get my man… errr, woman… errr, the wino!" Everyone guffawed again. I told them all, "Ok, I admit it, you all got me and got me good. Now, get that crap off my car!" More laughter.

CHAPTER 21 - ADVENTURES WITH RICK

What is that on your pants?

Rick Heinlin, mentioned earlier in this book, was one of my favorite officers to work with. He was a close friend. Still is. He had a great sense of humor and had a penchant for practical jokes like me and all my brothers. In fact, my whole family liked Rick and we sort of accepted him into our family as an honorary Garrett.

I got to know Rick and his wife Diana on a personal level. Diana like my own wife, was a dispatcher at WHPD. We would have cook-outs on our days off with them. They raised rabbits for food. Lynn and I would borrow a rabbit from time to time from them to use in our magic shows. It was like having a "rabbit library" where I could check out a rabbit for free and return it after my gig. I didn't have to feed it and Rick and Diana were happy to let their rabbits experience a little fame in show business before they eventually wound up on a plate as rabbit stew.

Late one night on midnight shift, I was telling Rick about a bum camp that I had found that was quite elaborate. It had tents and a make-shift structure made out of old wooden pallets and scrap cardboard they found in dumpsters. It was in a wooded area near a strip-mall. Rick wanted to see it for himself.

In between calls when the evening slowed down, Rick and I met up in the strip-mall parking lot and begun walking through the woods to the homeless encampment. After we arrived, we found it abandoned. We looked around a bit to make sure there wasn't anything illegal like drugs or weapons. We found nothing and walked back through the woods to our patrol cars.

Under the parking lot lights, we stood there a bit chatting when Rick glanced down and asked, "What is that on your pants?" I shined my flashlight down at my pant legs. IT WAS HUMAN FECES!

At some point of us traipsing through the woods, I had apparently stepped in wino poop. The poo transferred to my pant leg as I walked and it brushed against my shoe. I told Rick, "I've got to go to the PD and wash this mess off!"

I got in my patrol car and headed to the PD. I had to roll all my windows down because the smell was so powerful, it was starting to make me nauseous – and I have a really strong constitution.

I parked by the sally port area where there was a water spigot and hose attached to the building. Putting my thumb over the end of the hose to increase the water stream's pressure, I sprayed the bottom of my shoe and my lower pant leg. It pretty much all came off of my shoe, but the fabric of my uniform pants now wet from the water, retained poop remnants.

Rick had followed me to the police department to watch me, laugh at me some more, and revel in my stinky discomfort. After the hose didn't get it all off of my pants, we went into the building. His wife Diana was at the dispatcher window and asked, "What are you two up to now?" "Dale stepped in crap" Rick gleefully replied. I added, "Yeah and I washed it off and the smell is still there!"

Trying to help, Diana said, I have some perfume in my purse, do you want to spritz a little on it to see if it helps? I rationalized that poop plus perfume would balance each other out and it would be a neutral smell. I couldn't have been more wrong! The two scents together were unbearable. Rick and Diana both had an extended laugh at my odoriferous predicament.

I didn't want to have to go home to change and turn on lights because it was Lynn's day off and she was on an opposite shift. I knew I would wake her up, even though she's a heavy sleeper, but I was out of options.

I drove to my house with the windows down once again and went inside to change. Sure enough, I unintentionally woke Lynn up and naturally, she asked, "What are you doing." "I'm changing pants." "Why?" she sleepily asked. "Because there's poop on this pair." She didn't even ask how or why poop had gotten on my pants, she just pulled the cover over her head to block the light, rolled over, and went back to sleep.

Rick still laughs about my stinky misfortune to this day.

Stakeout

Some more off-duty work became available. A work building and barn belonging to the school board on the northeast side of town had been having almost nightly thefts from their open-air work garage and burglaries to their building.

Always in need of extra spending money, I volunteered for the plain-clothes detail. Since it was a two-man detail, Rick signed up too. Rick and I devised a plan. We planned to park a bicycle in the fenced perimeter of the building as our bait. Then we decided that we would hide in the building and watch and wait.

The night of the stakeout detail came. Someone gave us a ride to the location so there would be no out-of-place cars parked in the compound and we checked in on the radio to let them know we were actively at our special detail.

We parked the bike outside the building but within the locked fenced area that surrounded the property. Then, we discovered a problem. The windows of the building offered us a very limited view of the fenced compound. Since we didn't know from what direction our bad guy might come from, we needed to see all the way around the building and property.

We decided that if we got on top of the flat roofed, one-story building and laid down in a prone position, we would be concealed well enough from the ground level and could see everything we needed to see. But how were we going to get up there?

I don't remember which one of us it was, but one of us discovered that there was already a ladder leaning against the back of the building. It couldn't be any more perfect! So far, the stakeout gods were smiling upon us.

We climbed the ladder and laid down on the roof. Rick was dealing with some sort of inner ear issue at the time that affected his ability to hear well. Suddenly, his police radio went off as another officer was calling something in. It was really loud! I told Rick, "Turn that crap down! You're going to scare away our prey!"

Most stakeouts are long, boring, and uneventful. This one was none of that! We were not in position for more than ten minutes when we heard the eight-foot-tall chain-link fence rattle and saw a tall, thin male bounding over it as effortlessly as a gazelle. He was in the compound and had grabbed our bait bicycle!

Since only one of us could go down the ladder at one time, we quickly came up with a plan. I would go down the ladder and make the apprehension and he, gun drawn, would maintain visual on the suspect and cover me from the edge of the rooftop.

As I'm trying as fast as I can to shimmy down the ladder, Rick took a detour from the plan and started shouting for the bad guy to, "STOP! GET ON THE GROUND!" The guy looked up at him, shrugged and still pushing the bicycle, disappeared from Rick's view underneath a canopy.

Meanwhile, I'm hearing Rick screaming as I'm getting down the ladder while juggling my police radio in one hand and my flashlight in the other. Thinking that the suspect must be fleeing from us, I called dispatch and screamed "BACKUP, SEND US BACKUP!" Rick's radio was still turned down and he heard me shouting and interpreted it that the suspect was coming at me and I was telling HIM (the bad guy) to back up!

Being the loyal friend and partner he was, Rick decided that the fastest way to get down there and help me was to jump off the building! He holstered his pistol and did just that, fortunately landing in some soft sand.

By the time Rick made it around the building, I had Mr. bad guy on the ground at gunpoint and was effecting the arrest. We got him cuffed and transported to the jail in Bartow. We later learned that our bad guy was a minor league baseball player for a very high-profile team. Apparently, the minor leagues didn't pay their players enough back then to support their drug habits.

After the adrenaline rush was winding down, Rick and I high-fived and were elated at our capture. It was even more special because we were good friends and we had done it together. It was like a real life "buddy-cop" movie.

Rick later retired from WHPD and moved to Nashville, Tennessee where at the time of this writing, is a detective with the Nashville Police Department and is just a few years away from his second retirement. We still regularly stay in contact with each other to this day.

CHAPTER 22 - FAMILY WAR STORIES

Gary the K-9 officer

With six of us Garretts working at the same police department and working in different divisions, on various, rotating shifts, it was rare that all of us were off at the same time and could get together for a family meal or a cookout.

It however, did happen occasionally. Gary, Gary's wife Lindy, and myself were in the patrol division, Lynn, my wife was in communications, Carl was in the motorcycle division, and Carl's wife, Kelly, was a community service officer. With that many people in the same profession getting together, conversations more often than not, naturally turned to war stories and funny things each of us encountered during our shifts.

During one of our family meals, Gary shared a unique capture of some prowlers that he had been looking for. He was dispatched around 10:30 PM one evening to a middle-class neighborhood on the southwest side of the city in regards to three teenage boys loitering in the area and possibly attempting to break into parked cars. When he arrived, he performed a cursory check of the area but didn't find anyone on foot that looked out of place or suspicious.

He made contact with the person who had called in the complaint and learned a little more about what the three boys were wearing and which direction she had last seen them walking.

In Winter Haven, there are fifty-five lakes of various sizes. Ten of those lakes are connected by canals and create what is called, "The Chain of Lakes." So, most subdivisions and neighborhoods are never far from a body of water.

Gary began to patrol toward Lake Shipp in search of the three prowlers. Suddenly, he spotted them about the same time they spotted him and they took off running toward Lake Shipp. Gary's patrol car was facing the opposite way from the direction that they had run. It took him a bit to turn around, giving the three ne'er-do-wells a small head start.

Just as Gary rounded the corner in his patrol car, he saw the three boys run into the edge of the water hiding among some thick brush and cattails. Gary pulled his unit off the road so that his headlights were shining on the area where the boys were hiding.

He got out of his car and on his unit's public address loudspeaker, ordered the boys to exit the water and come to the patrol car. He said, "You all have about 15 seconds before I release my K-9. You will be bitten unless you come out now and surrender!" The boys could hear the vicious barks from the police dog and within about ten seconds, they all came trudging out of the edge of the lake holding their hands high in the air.

I should remind you at this point that Gary was in the patrol division – same as me. He was NOT in the K-9 unit. Gary searched them and put them in the back seat of his patrol car. One of the boys asked, "Hey, where's the K-9?" Gary replied, "What K-9?"

After he had given them the order to exit the water or be bitten by the police dog, he had lowered the microphone down by his leg and did his best vocal impression of a vicious, blood-thirsty police K-9 barking. It was a good enough bluff to convince them to all give up peacefully and Gary added, "and I didn't even have to get my boots wet!" We all had a good laugh from that one!

Wet and naked

Gary's lake related story triggered one of my own. Florida, 99% of the time is mild to warm. Heck, most of the time it's just down-right hot!

On this particular January night however, the temps had fallen to the lower 40s. That's bitterly cold to us Floridians! I was working midnight shift in the north west quadrant of the city. Another officer pulled over a car in my zone so I thought I'd drive by to act as back-up.

Before I arrived, the guy bolted away from the officer and sprinted down a small inclined driveway next to a closed business toward Lake Cannon. Perhaps it was the alcohol doing his thinking for him or the fact he had outstanding warrants for his arrest that he decided his best course of action to evade capture was to make a swim for it. He darted away and splashed into the lake, swimming about twenty yards from the shore.

The other officer, Mike Tibbs was able to commandeer a small boat for us to use to go out on the lake and save this fool from drowning. By now, our supervisor, Sergeant Roger Quails had arrived to oversee "Operation Retrieve The Wet Guy."

He waited on shore while Mike and I hopped into the small boat and started moving out toward our impromptu swimmer. He swam away from us and further out into the lake. Now about seventy-five or a hundred yards offshore, Mike and I were able to see with our flashlights that he had removed his shirt. I presume to prevent the water-soaked fabric from weighing him down.

We spent at least fifteen minutes trying to convince him to get up in the boat with us. We warned him about the alligators in the area. In fact, I could hear one in the distance making that familiar grunt that gators make and brought his attention to the sound.

There are alligators in almost every lake in Florida. They're so common in fact, they even taught us how to wrangle an alligator in the police academy. I bet that's a section of police academy training that is exclusive to Florida. I've told other officers from other states about it and they thought I was pulling their leg. I wasn't.

Now exhausted from the swimming and treading water, the goofball decided that giving up was better than drowning or worse yet, being chomped on by an alligator. As Mike and I pulled him into the boat to handcuff him, we saw that not only had he removed his shirt, but every other stitch of clothing he had been wearing to include his underwear! The dude was butt-naked! I handcuffed Mr. Wet N' Slippery while Mike maneuvered the boat to shore.

Once we got to shore, Sergeant Quails and I each grabbed an arm and escorted the bare-naked prisoner to where our patrol cars were at the other end of that long driveway while Mike returned the boat to the nearby owner.

As I said earlier, it was bitterly cold that night. Now I don't know how much you might know about human anatomy, but when a man is cold, it's common for his winky-dinky to shrink to an unusually small size. As we're escorting him on the walk up that long driveway, I look down and noticed that fact and couldn't help but say something about it, teasing our prisoner for being hung like a toddler.

Sergeant Quails laughed at my comments and later told me, "I can't believe you made fun of that fella's manhood! You know if you were in the same situation, you would have shrunk up too!" I replied, "Perhaps, but I've got better sense than to go skinny dipping in cold weather like this!" There was laughter from

Sergeant Quails and laughter from my family as I related this story to them.

Ironically, that's not the only wet naked man I ever had occasion to fish out of an area lake. My brother Carl and I were both off-duty and assisted other officers in capturing another wet, naked, slippery guy out of chest high water who was hiding in some high cattails near the lake's edge.

Other than us volunteering to go in after him because we were in our street clothes so the other officers didn't have to get their uniforms wet, I don't remember too many details on this one. But I do however, remember diligently watching our backs for any approaching alligators.

Carl's special delivery

During their careers, many police officers find themselves in situations where a woman is giving birth and the ambulance isn't there yet. With no medically trained personnel around, the officer on scene finds themselves playing the role of midwife.

This incident occurred before Carl was a motor officer. He was in the patrol division and was working on the dayshift. Dayshifts were typically pretty quiet. The bulk of the calls on dayshift were from people discovering that a crime such as a criminal mischief, theft, or burglary had been committed during the overnight hours and they would want to report the crime and have a police report made.

At a little after 8:00 AM, Carl was dispatched to an obstetrician's office in the downtown area of the city in regards to a burglary. When Carl arrived, he entered through the front entrance and through the lobby that he said was almost full of pregnant women awaiting their appointments.

He met the doctor and the doctor explained that when he and his nurses showed up to work that morning, he found his office trashed and whoever did it had climbed up on his desk and had defecated. Carl asked, "Is there anything missing?" The doctor replied. "That's the weird part, other than this stuff knocked off my desk and office shelves, and this poop on my desk, we can't seem to find anything missing."

Carl looked closer at the pile of relatively fresh excrement on the doctor's desk and said, "I don't think we're dealing with a burglary here. At least not by a human anyway. This scat looks too small to be human feces. I think you may have a critter of some sort getting in." Carl instructed the doctor and the nurses to fan out and check each storeroom, closet, and exam room. He told them to carefully look for any holes in the wall, floor, or ceiling where a critter such as a squirrel or raccoon could have made entry.

The nurses began searching while Carl and the doctor also started inspecting the doctor's office. Within twenty seconds, Carl said he heard a blood curdling scream come from one of the exam rooms. When he and the doctor ran to investigate, Carl said the nurse was backed up tightly against the wall, becoming one with the paint, pointing, and almost unable to even speak because of her terror! He looked in the direction she was pointing and said the biggest possum he had ever seen was standing on its hind legs on a counter, baring his teeth and hissing loudly! The nurse squeezed by Carl and the doctor and went running to safety!

Carl told the doctor "Wait here and don't let him get out of the exam room!" Carl just so happened to have a snare pole like dog catchers use in the trunk of his patrol car. He jogged through the lobby full of pregnant women, retrieved the snare pole from his car, and ran back through the lobby. He said he noticed looks of concern and bewilderment on the ladies faces as he rushed by them on his way back to the exam room!

When he got to the exam room, the possum with the nasty attitude had made his way to the floor. After a couple failed attempts, Carl was able to lasso it. Then began the struggle to get him outside, and that angry, angry possum did NOT want to go peacefully. Carl wrestled it down the hall and opened the door leading to the lobby, pulling the giant marsupial into sight of the now screaming patients. After their initial screams, Carl looked at them all and said, "NEXT!" I don't think any of them had ever contemplated that method of giving birth!

As he continued to wrestle the possum through the lobby, he said all the women were still squealing and drawing their feet up off the floor as best they could with their big pregnant bellies in the way!

What a great story! The whole family laughed out loud once again! If there's one thing I can say about our Garrett family get togethers, it's that they were/are always entertaining!

Family team work

This is a family war story that I fondly remember every year around the Christmas season. When this particular event took place, Lynn and I were both working on the dayshift and it was two days before Christmas.

Lynn took a frantic 911 call from a young child. He exclaimed on the phone to her that, "Somebody stole Christmas!" After a few more questions, she understood that someone had broken into the child's home and stolen all the Christmas presents from under their tree. When she asked to speak to the child's parent, the little boy said, "Mamma can't talk on the phone right now, she's crying."

The articulate young African American boy was able to tell Lynn their address and it was in my assigned zone. I was dispatched to the call of a burglary already occurred. The house was in a not-so-good part of town.

When I pulled up in front of the house, the same little six-year-old boy came running toward me as I was exiting my patrol car. He said the same thing he had told to Lynn on the phone, "Somebody stole Christmas!" I followed him inside where I met his mother, a single mom. She was sitting on the worn-out couch, sobbing.

The scarcely decorated four-foot-tall Christmas tree that looked like it came from a second-hand thrift store was completely void of presents underneath. She managed to speak through her tears that she had scrimped and saved for three months to be able to afford at least one present for each of her three children, and now it was all gone with Christmas only two days away.

It broke my heart. I took her information and a description of the presents that were stolen from under the tree for my report and hurriedly left before they witnessed my own eyes tearing up.

The rest of the day, I couldn't stop thinking about that call. As I patrolled, every Christmas decoration I saw and every child that I saw reminded me of that little boy, his siblings, and their heartbroken mother.

When Lynn and I got off work, I told her more about that call and how poor the family appeared and how devastated those children were. I told her about their mother too and how she was disappointed that Christmas was coming and she had to explain to them that they were not going to be getting any presents this year.

I couldn't let this stand. Lynn and I hopped in our car and drove over to my brother Carl's house. I explained the situation and told him that we needed to do something for this family. He agreed. I spoke to my brother Gary too and it struck a chord in him as well. We pooled our money together and the next day, Christmas Eve, we all braved the crowds of shoppers at the department store and went on a shopping spree with that pooled money.

Using the information from a copy of my police report, we bought all the same toys that the mom had reported to me as stolen. We still had almost $250.00 left over, so we continued to stack other toys in our cart until it was overflowing. Lynn even picked out a nice necklace from the jewelry department for the mom.

After we checked out, we went back to Carl's house where we all sat around his dining room table wrapping all the presents. It was like Santa's workshop with the sounds of scissors snapping, tape being dispensed, and Christmas paper scraps flying all over the place as our family carefully wrapped all of the presents.

By the time we were finished it was about 5:00 PM Christmas Eve. We loaded all the presents up into two cars and we drove to the family's house. I walked up to the door alone while my family waited in the cars.

It took them a moment to recognize me since I wasn't in my police uniform. I told the mom that ever since I had taken the report from her the day before, I couldn't stop thinking about their situation and with her permission, my family and I would like to help her out and save Christmas for her children.

With tears in her eyes, she agreed. I stepped back outside and waved my family in. Like a parade of Christmas elves, they all carried armloads of presents into the house and placed them around the tree – almost obscuring the small tree itself from view! I handed her the wrapped necklace and told her that Santa told me to tell her that this one was for her. With tears in her eyes, she thanked me over and over and over again and hugged my neck. She said, "God bless you. God bless you all!"

God did bless us. The feelings we got from being able to salvage Christmas for this poor mom who worked so hard at two jobs to provide for her family was our pleasure. And to save those kids from waking up Christmas morning with not a single gift to open was our blessing. It was probably the best Christmas that family ever had and you know what? It was the best one I ever had as well.

CHAPTER 23 - DARE TO BE DIFFERENT

The new guy has arrived

One of the interesting things about law enforcement is that there are many jobs available within the job itself. For example, there's patrol division, motorcycle division, air patrol, narcotics division, crime scene tech unit, detective division, horse mounted patrol division, crime prevention, school resource and DARE divisions, and others. There are many spokes that make the law enforcement "wheel" operate properly.

I showed up to work one day and went to my department mailbox before briefing like I did every day. This time however, there was something in my box that changed the course of my career. A department-wide memo had been put in everyone's mailbox announcing the position of a DARE (Drug Abuse Resistance Education) officer had come available and encouraged all who were interested to say so in writing to the department's head, Captain J.J. Staten via their chain of command. The DARE program was a prevention-based, 17-week, structured curriculum taught by a uniformed police officer to elementary aged children in their schools.

I had been in patrol for a long while and thought this is something I was definitely interested in. I thought to myself that my ability to relate to kids along with the magic tricks I performed would be perfect for disseminating an anti-drug message to children.

The department already had one DARE officer, Donna Reed. She was the department's first DARE officer and had done an admirable job. However, a year before, she was involved in an auto accident and was in constant pain. She knew that she wasn't able to do the job like she once did because of her injuries and the city was giving her a hard time about getting a medical retirement. When they posted the announcement for the second DARE officer, I'm not sure if the position was meant to supplement Donna's workload or replace it completely since she was actively seeking a medical retirement.

I wrote a well worded memo to Captain Staten declaring my interest in the DARE position. I don't know how many applicants they had, but the position came down to just two people, myself and a female officer named Sarah Johnson who I mentioned earlier in this book. Sarah had a college degree in education. She could have easily been an elementary school teacher with that degree. I didn't have a degree at all. In fact, I had no college at all except for my time going through the police academy and some training classes that I had attended. But what I did have was a secret weapon. MAGIC!

On the day of the interviews, Sarah had hers first. I saw her in the hall when she came out and asked her how it went. She replied that it had gone pretty well and she was hopeful.

Now, it was time for MY interview. I didn't go into the interview empty handed. I carried what's commonly called a "catalog case" with me. They asked me all the standard questions and then asked me what I thought that I could bring to the position that my competitors couldn't. For the next ten to fifteen minutes, I went into performer mode. I pulled magic effects out of my case that not only had great entertainment value, but very strong anti-drug messages as well.

The interviewers had all seen me perform before at the

department's Christmas parties. But I don't think they realized until that interview how magic and entertainment could be utilized along with some showmanship to convey positive, anti-drug messages to kids. I blew them away. I was confident that I had done everything I could in the interview but in the back of my mind, I knew I was going up against a formidable opponent with a four-year teaching degree.

Within just a few days, another department-wide memo went out announcing that a new DARE Officer had been selected. The position went to ME! I was thrilled! I had so many ideas bouncing around in my head about how I could use my magic to enhance the curriculum that I would be teaching. It was an exciting time!

Before I could be a certified DARE Officer though, I had to go to DARE Officer Training. The two-week training was conducted in Sarasota, Florida about 95 miles away from Winter Haven which meant I would be staying in Sarasota for two weeks until my training was complete. But I only stayed one week.

The weekend after the first week of training, a major hurricane was bearing down on Florida. It was Hurricane Andrew. Andrew was a Category Five storm that destroyed large swaths of South Florida, wiping out whole neighborhoods and causing $26.5 billion in damage. It was the most expensive hurricane damage amount on record at the time.

The remainder of the training would have to take place at some point in the future when the state was able to re-group and start getting back to normal. I went back home and temporarily back into patrol until the second week of training in Sarasota resumed about a month later.

The DARE Officer training changed me. I had never been much of a drinker but would keep a few wine coolers on hand from time to time. When I returned after that second week of training, I asked

Lynn, "Are you going to drink those wine coolers in the fridge?" She replied, they've been in there a while, probably not." I walked into the kitchen, retrieved them from the refrigerator and poured them down the sink. Lynn asked me, "What are you doing that for?" I replied, "I can't very well preach to children about avoiding alcohol if I drink it myself. It just seems hypocritical." Lynn shrugged and said, "OK."

When I went back to work on Monday morning, as an official certified DARE Officer, I was assigned a desk in my own office in a police department annex building next to the city's tennis courts. My desk was directly across from Donna's desk.

One of the first things I noticed was that our division was way behind other departments in the drug displays, updated pamphlets for citizens, and other crime prevention type supplies. Some of the flyers looked like they were designed in the early 1970's. I didn't really blame Donna. It had been a long while since she herself went to DARE Officer training and wasn't as current on things as I was. Plus, she was dealing with her daily pain from her injuries and just didn't feel like making changes in our division.

Over the next several months, I presented idea after idea to my supervisor, Kathy Mannet who had also come over from patrol. She loved my proposals and when I would approach her with an idea or an asset that I thought would enhance our anti-drug displays at community events she would say, "Sounds good, let's run it up the chain of command!" Off we would go right that moment to Lieutenant Fred Deleon's office. He usually rubber stamped my idea so off we would go to Captain J.J. Staten's office. J.J. always loved the ideas too, so off to the Chief's office we would go.

Kathy and I would sit in the Chief's outer office excitedly telling the Chief's secretary, Carol about my new innovative idea. Once

Chief Marken was through with his call or whoever he was meeting with, Carol would get us in to see him and he would usually reflect on it a moment and then approve the idea!

This scenario repeated itself over and over again until I had gotten the department updated anti-drug displays, fresh literature to hand out to citizens, a McGruff the crime dog costume, our DARE cars marked up as official DARE patrol cars that set them apart from the regular patrol units, and much, much more!

I was an energetic go-getter and was able to get things accomplished because of a great, supportive sergeant, lieutenant, captain, and chief. It was the perfect team effort and things were going along swimmingly! I was excited to go to work every day and thoroughly enjoyed using my magic tricks to entertain and educate the kids. I was able to actually combine both of my loves – magic and law enforcement! I couldn't have dreamed of a more perfect career situation!

The Haunted Crack House

Donna was finally granted her medical retirement and left the department. I had the office all to myself. That sounds like a good thing, but it also meant that I was now responsible for all of the elementary schools within the city's jurisdiction.

The DARE program's structured curriculum is designed for the students at the fifth-grade level. In our spare time though, DARE officers are directed to do classroom visitations for the other grade levels as well. This was too much work for one person. But I never complained. I enjoyed staying busy.

Even though I liked being on the go to all of the elementary schools in our jurisdiction, I couldn't get to all the grade levels. Plus, there was a brand-new DARE curriculum coming down the pike for middle school aged students. It was time to give me a new DARE partner. The officer selected for the position was Terry Brownden. Terry and I got along famously.

I taught him the ropes of issuing curriculum materials to the kids, scheduling meetings with teachers, ordering DARE supplies, putting together teaching schedules, and organizing our multi-school DARE graduations that had grown into spectacular, very large events attended by city officials like the mayor and some celebrity guests as well. Terry and I made a GREAT team! He was gung-ho about making our division the best it could be just like I was. Although I taught him everything that I knew about running a successful DARE program, I didn't teach him any magic tricks. That was MY schtick.

Every year at Halloween, a local civic club would operate a haunted house. They used an empty store space at the mall that was formerly a video game room. In recent years however, their attendance had started to diminish. They pretty much did the same thing year after year and people were bored with it.

When Terry and I returned from a National DARE Officers conference In Houston, Texas, we came home with a brand-new idea that another department had done at their then closed down jail. They called it "The Haunted Crack House." When the fellow DARE Officer in Houston told us about it, I immediately thought of the haunted house held every year by the local civic club in Winter Haven.

Another trip up the chain of command and there I sat in the Chief's outer office again, excitedly telling his secretary Carol about my crazy idea. A haunted house with anti-drug themed scenes mixed in with the civic club's standard scenes of typical horror and mayhem.

The Chief green-lighted the idea! Our next step was to convince the civic club to allow us to infiltrate their yearly fund raiser.

Terry and I met with their president and explained the concept. We told them with Terry and I both promoting it in all of the elementary schools along with the family friendly endorsement of the police department, their haunted house would be bigger, better, and more profitable than it had been in many years.

We didn't even want any of their admission money. We just wanted an opportunity to present an anti-drug message in an exciting, fresh, new way to the public. It would not only breathe new life into their yearly project, but give the police department a highly visible public relations boost as well. It was a win-win proposition!

Their club approved it! In early September, construction on the interior of The Haunted Crack House began. The police department had four scenes in the haunted house while the civic club had about six. We also enlisted the talents of an artist to draw a mural on the building's exterior emblazoned with the name of the attraction, "The Haunted Crack House" along with spooky scenes and anti-drug slogans. Terry and I along with the newly hired crime prevention officer, Jim Vanderfield, School Resource Officers Mike Tibbs and Phil Younger, Officer Shane Dibby, and a few other volunteers painted in the details of the mural.

The scenes Terry and I came up with were a graveyard scene with tombstones of people who had died from using various drugs. The tombstones depicted their drugs of choice.

The second scene we did was a casket we were able to get loaned to us by a local funeral home. It contained a uniformed, helmet wearing high school football player and was littered with empty beer cans. I wrote a script for the person conducting the tour about how the football player had died after his game when he decided to drink and drive. Of course, as people began to exit the room, the football player would sit up in the casket and grab at the tour groups to give them a fright.

The third scene we did was a courtroom scene. The tour group stood in the center of the room as a scare actor playing a judge wearing a real judge's robe that we borrowed from an actual judge in Bartow (our county seat), passed sentence on a murderous drug dealer.

A small room behind the tour group then lit up and an inmate was in an electric chair. The executioner threw the switch. Thanks to my special effects magic trick I contributed, sparks flew from the switch box and a strobe light activated. The inmate wearing an actual inmate uniform we borrowed from the Polk County Jail began to convulse as though he was being electrocuted and then slumped over in the chair. As the group was being ushered into the next scene, the inmate came back to life, tore loose from the chair and banged loudly on the plexiglass wall separating him from the tour group to hasten their exit.

The most difficult to find prop for this scene was a realistic looking electric chair. Since nothing even close was commercially available, our crime prevention officer, Jim Vanderfield and I spent two days on the patio of my apartment - building the realistic looking electric chair from photographs of an actual electric chair I had researched at the library.
It looked identical to Florida's ominously named electric chair, "Ole Sparky." After the last year we did the Haunted Crack House, I wound up with the electric chair. It sat in my living room for several years and was occasionally used as a regular chair when we had a lot of company at our house for parties. It was definitely a conversation starter!

The department's fourth and final scene was one I called "The Grimm Reefer." Tour groups would enter a room with blacklights and see a 6-foot-long marijuana cigarette and a huge syringe hanging from the ceiling. The script I wrote for the tour guide was about how sometimes, marijuana could act as a gateway drug to harder more deadly drugs that were just waiting around the corner to take their life. An actor wearing a Grimm Reaper (Reefer) costume emerged from the shadows to scare the group into the civic club's finale scene where they were chased out of the exit by a chainsaw wielding lunatic.

In addition to the scenes inside the Haunted Crack House, I arranged for a local wrecker service to tow a wrecked car with extensive roll-over damage to the parking lot right outside the Haunted Crack House to underscore the dangers of driving impaired. Crime scene tape surrounding the wreck complimented the mock carnage. Along with our patrol cars sitting on either end of the wrecked car with our blue lights going, it was quite a beacon to attract people driving by and mall shoppers to come tour the Haunted Crack House.

We also set up a table outside on the sidewalk with our new anti-drug displays and updated anti-drug literature I had procured for the citizens to take free of charge.

Many, many of our DARE students came out to the event and loved hanging out with us and asking Terry and I questions about drugs and being a police officer away from the school classroom environment where there just wasn't that much time for such social interaction with us.

The parents of the kids also enjoyed meeting us and a lot of them told us how much their children loved DARE class and their DARE officer. Some shook my hand and told me, "My kid talks about you all the time. It's good to actually meet you in person myself!" It was very rewarding to know how much of an impact we were having on the children of our community.

The Haunted Crack House was a fun, extremely successful public relations tool that garnered the department a lot of positive coverage from the local media while providing a wonderful public relations opportunity. Sgt. Mannet, Lt. Deleon, Capt. Staten, and Chief Marken all loved the execution of the concept I had brought to them and they still mention it occasionally to this day.

CHAPTER 24 - MY EYES ARE WATERING

A father/son talk

As part of the DARE curriculum, my students were required to do various projects in DARE workbooks that were issued to them. They wrote their name on the front of their workbooks and everyone would clamor to get to assist me at the beginning of each of my weekly visits to be the one to hand out the workbooks to their classmates.

Most of the time, there was time for the students to complete their assignments in their workbooks during my hour-long classroom visit. A few lessons however, required them to write an essay or do more work by the time I returned for the next lesson in a week.

One week, when I arrived to teach my class, the teacher pulled me aside and told me that she caught one of the students, Charlie, copying his DARE essay from another student's workbook. I was surprised as Charlie was one of the most attentive, friendly, and engaged kids in the class when I would come there to teach. He had become one of my favorite students. I thanked her for letting me know and told her I'd like to talk to Charlie after today's class if it was ok. She agreed and I taught the lesson I was there to teach.

As I packed my briefcase to leave, I said, "Charlie, I'd like to speak with you for a moment outside please." Charlie stood up from his desk and followed me to the sidewalk just outside his classroom.

Now, I have never had children myself, but I had a father who could hurt me very effectively if I did something wrong. I'm not talking physically. I'm talking emotionally. When I would do something that displeased him, he would sit me down and express how disappointed he was in me. This to me, was crushing. Disappointing my father was the last thing I ever wanted to do because I respected him so much. I knew that Charlie respected me in the same way.

So, using my own father's weapon of choice, I told Charlie, "I know that you cheated and copied another person's workbook." Then I dropped the dad bomb on him. I put my hand on his shoulder and said, "Charlie, I really thought you respected me both as a police officer and as a human. I am very disappointed in you."

His tears began to well up and then roll down his little cheeks. My dad's technique worked! Charlie apologized profusely and said that he would re-write his essay and make me proud of him again. I told him, "I've always been proud of you. You're the most attentive student in class. But cheating? Charlie, this is what has really upset me."

Again, he promised to do better and make it right and to never cheat again. To my knowledge, he never did. Out of all his classmates, he wrote the longest, most heartfelt anti-drug essay I had ever seen. In it, he promised over and over never to do drugs, to work hard, and to always be honest with people.

Years later after I had retired, Lynn and I were out to dinner at a steakhouse in town. There was a small issue with our meal. I didn't really complain, but I just let the waitress know about it so no other customers experienced the same problem. I didn't ask for anything to be re-cooked or for my money back. I just let her know about the issue as a courtesy.

Apparently at this restaurant chain, they had a policy that if any customer made any type of complaint to the waitress, they had to inform the manager who would then come to your table personally to make whatever was wrong, right again and smooth things over.

I looked up and the manager was CHARLIE! All grown up now, he had worked his way up to management at this restaurant. I told him how proud I was of him and his success in the restaurant business. He shook my hand and thanked me for the lessons I had taught him way back in elementary school about saying no to drugs and especially about being honest. He still remembered that brief father/son like chat we had all those years ago on the sidewalk outside of his classroom. We chatted for a little while and he left our table to attend to other matters.

When Lynn and I were ready to go, we waited for quite a while for our waitress to bring our check to us. Finally, I caught her attention and waved her over to request our bill. She smiled and said, "Oh, you guys are all set. Charlie took care of your whole meal!" I was flabbergasted but also humbled. All those years later and Charlie still wanted to do something to please me and make amends for cheating on his DARE essay in the fifth grade.

You were a good kid Charlie. And you grew up to be a fine young man. I didn't see you that night to thank you personally for the meal. If you ever read this book, know that my wife and I thank you and I'm so very proud of the man you became.

CHAPTER 25 – THE UGLINESS I CAN'T UNSEE

Before you read any further, I should warn you that in this chapter of the book, I'm going to describe things that may make you lose your appetite. If it's almost mealtime when you're reading this, you might want to put the book down and come back to it a little later. If you have a weak stomach, you may want to skip this chapter in its entirety. I've kept these particular stories a bit brief intentionally.

Barbed wire

Being a police officer was both fun and exciting. But there's a part of the job that the general public doesn't even think about. There are many of my vivid memories that have still not gone away after forty years. I used to have regular nightmares about some of the things I'm about to describe. But as time marched on, the dreams have fortunately decreased to the point of being almost nonexistent. These are just a few of these types of things I witnessed during my career. There were many others.

This first incident I want to share with you involved a man who owned a sprawling ranch in the Lake Wales area. For months he had experienced issues with trespassers riding four-wheel all-terrain vehicles on his property. Posting no trespassing signs did no good. The riders would ignore the signs and continued to ride and trespass on his hilly property.

He decided that he needed to fence off his property with a barbed wire fence to keep out the trespassers - which he had every right to do. The very next weekend, the four-wheelers were back again. This time, when the lead four-wheeler crested a hill at a fast rate of speed, he struck the barbed wire fence.

He didn't hit it head-on. He hit the fence at an angle. The fourteen-year-old boy riding the ATV was thrown from his seat and physically slid down about a ten-foot stretch of the fence. The barbs on the wire shredded him. He had an uncountable number of deep gashes from his knees up to his face. When I arrived at the scene, he was covered in blood and still screaming out in agony. He eventually passed out from the pain.

The ambulance arrived after a while and transported him to the emergency room. Just as I'm sure that boy who is now a man still bears the physical scars of that day, I still bear the mental scars of seeing him in such agony and not being able to do anything to stop his pain.

The not-so well-being check

I was on day shift. It was a beautiful Sunday morning. I was dispatched to a house that was situated next to a city park on the north-west side of Winter Haven. The call was a well-being check. The 40-year-old man who lived at that house was distraught and suicidal. He had been talking to his sister on the telephone and she was very concerned when they hung up with each other about his mental state. So, she contacted the police department for us to go by and check on him.

I had just driven past Inman Park so I was very close by when I was dispatched on the call. When I arrived at the house, I knocked on the door and there was no response. I banged on the door and there was no response. I shouted, "Winter Haven Police Department!" There was no response. I stepped off the porch and decided to walk around the house to see if I could see anyone through any of the windows.

When I got to a bedroom window, the curtain was opened just slightly. I peered into the room and could see two human feet laying on the floor. The rest of the person was obscured by the bed. I banged on the window, but got no response. Fearing that the person inside was in need of urgent medical assistance, I went back around front and kicked open the front door. I made my way through the house to the bedroom where I had seen his feet. What I saw next was horrifying.

The distraught man had in fact committed suicide. He had placed a shotgun under his chin and pulled the trigger. The scene looked like something you would see in a horror movie. But this wasn't a movie. It was very real.

The blast violently tore the top half of the man's head completely off. Blood was all over the wall and ceiling of the room. Bits of brain matter were stuck to the ceiling and some of it was still loosening and splattering to the floor. It's an image that I will never forget. It still bothers me to this day and has over the years been the subject of more than a few of my nightmares.

The battery

I was dispatched as back-up for my brother Carl who was a motorcycle officer and a traffic homicide investigator. It was a serious single vehicle accident on Lucerne Park Road in north-east Winter Haven.

The car had obviously been traveling at a very high rate of speed. It had gone airborne and struck a tree. The impact bent the entire front end of the car backward toward the passenger compartment. The car came to rest at an extreme angle against the tree. The driver had died on impact.

Carl and I got there at about the same time. We approached the driver's side of the car and could see the deceased driver slumped over toward the window. The windshield of the car had been completely smashed out during the impact. Fluids from the engine were dripping into the passenger compartment of the vehicle. One of the fluids was the acid from the cracked car battery. It was dripping onto the driver's face. His skin was being chemically burned by each drip of the battery acid and small wisps of smoke rose from his face that was now taking on the features of a horribly disfigured Halloween mask. The smell was metallic and disgusting. There was nothing we could do for him. One doesn't easily forget seeing something like that.

The rice story

I was dispatched early on a Monday morning to an abandoned vehicle call in a citrus grove just outside of Lake Wales. Many times, people would steal vehicles, drive them into an orange grove, strip the vehicle, and then sell the parts. I figured that was also probably the case this time. I was wrong.

When I arrived, the crew leader of some migrant workers met me at the road and walked me through the grove where he had spotted the small pick-up truck. He said, "I didn't get close to it. I didn't want to mess up any tire tracks or footprints around it for you guys." I thanked him for being so thoughtful and once the vehicle was in my line of sight, continued by myself to walk up to it.

What I saw next was a gruesome sight. There was a garden hose coming out of the tailpipe and the other end was in the driver's side window. I looked through the window glass and saw a dead man. He had been there for several days. Flies were flying in and out of the window. The man's body was in an advanced stage of decomposition.

He was wearing a newer pair of jeans and I could literally see his pants moving. The movement was being caused by maggots that were devouring his body. Focusing my attention on his face, I could also see maggots in his nostrils, eye sockets, and saw a few larvae falling from the corner of his open mouth. He was a white male, but his skin had started turning black as his flesh rotted.

I have a strong stomach and had seen death many other times during my career. It didn't make me sick or even nauseous then. But this particular incident has stuck in my brain ever since. Even now, when I go to a Chinese or Japanese restaurant, I still can't eat white rice because it reminds me of this ghastly scene and those maggots both crawling in and falling from that man's mouth.

I'm telling you about these incidents not to "gross you out" but to remind you that when you see a police officer to remember that he or she has seen things that permanently affected them mentally. Be kind to them.

Some, including myself suffer from various levels of PTSD ranging from very, very mild like in my own case to extreme in others. Just like a war-time soldier, police officers see terrible things during their careers that the general public can't begin to fathom.

I credit comedy and performing magic for providing me my much-needed mental balance. It was a positive outlet for me. Being able to make people laugh and bring them joy was cathartic.

Some people aren't fortunate enough to have a hobby or an outlet like I did. I have personally known a few officers whose mental scars drove them to alcoholism and a few committed suicides themselves because the images of child abuse, gore, and death they witnessed in the line of duty wouldn't leave their heads.

If you know a police officer (or anyone for that matter) who is suffering from depression – or you yourself are experiencing dark thoughts, please put this book down right this moment and get help. The phone number for the suicide prevention hotline is 1-800-273-8255 or 988 from your mobile phone.

CHAPTER 26 - WHAT IS THAT SMELL!?

Well, after that last chapter, it's time to lighten the mood. As I near the end of this book, I couldn't resist telling you about one more prank. Although I unwittingly had a hand in it, it was my brother Carl who was the perpetrator this time.

My DARE partner Terry and I received word one day that the city was going to be closing the police annex building next to the public tennis courts. Well, not as much closing it, but repurposing it. Our offices would be moved to an area of the police department's main building that was formerly occupied by the detective division. The detectives all moved their offices to their own annex building near the National Guard Armory building.

So, moving day came toward the end of summer. That was great for Terry and I because school had not started yet and we were able to shuffle our summer schedule around to accommodate the move. Plus, Jim Vanderfield, our crime prevention officer was going to also get one of the three desks in the same office so he helped us move.

As we were settling in and getting all of our displays and supplies stored away in our new office, my brother Carl wandered through our work area. The motorcycle officers shared an office in the main building as well. He stopped at my desk to shoot the breeze for a few minutes.

As we were talking, he looked down on my desk at some of the supplies I had not yet put away and asked, "What's that?" He gestured toward a package of 15 or 20 green cookie looking disks on my desk. I told him, "Oh, that's something relatively new that we got for anti-drug seminars that we do for parents and grandparents. You light these cookies and they produce smoke with the exact smell of marijuana. It's to teach folks what to be on the look-out for if they suspect their kids or grandkids of using marijuana."

Carl asked, "It's not real marijuana?" I replied, "No, it's all synthetic. There's no THC in them, but when they burn, they smell like the real deal! It's like marijuana scented incense." Then he asked, "Can you spare a few of them?" I said, "Sure, but what are you going to do with them?" Then I quickly added, "Never mind, I probably don't want to know!" I handed him a couple of the synthetic marijuana disks and he happily went on his way.

About an hour or so later, Terry and I had to leave the building to attend a meeting. When we returned, the administration was all atwitter! All the brass was stomping up and down the halls attempting to find where the smell of marijuana was coming from. The smell was permeating the building!

They were all worked up in a state of agitation that an officer or civilian police employee would have the audacity to fire up a doobie within the walls of a police building! Carl sat in the motorman's office and could hear different members of the administration saying, "Is that smell what I think it is!?" And, "Where is it coming from!?" Carl lowered his head pretending to be doing paperwork while he stifled his laughter. He was reveling in being able to bear witness to the pay-off of his prank.

Of course, I knew immediately what caused the smell and exactly who was responsible, but I kept my mouth closed. A) to keep my brother out of trouble for a harmless prank, and B) to keep myself out of trouble for supplying him the means to pull off the prank.

At my first opportunity, I pulled Carl aside and asked, "Why did you do that in the building!? You could have gotten us BOTH in trouble!" Carl replied, "I didn't do it in the building. I took it outside right next to the air conditioner intake." I replied, "Geez Carl! I guess that explains why nobody could pinpoint where the smell was coming from. It was coming from every room in the building that had an AC vent!" We quietly laughed at his very successful, awesome prank.

None of the brass or anyone else at the department – outside of our own family - ever knew what had happened or exactly where the strong marijuana smell had come from. I guess if they read this book, they know now.

By the way, I never used those disks at public seminars after that. If a ranking officer from the east end of the building happened to attend the seminar and saw it and smelled it, it would have been way too easy for them to put two and two together and blame me for the shenanigans that Carl perpetrated. I would go as far as keeping my mouth shut, but I wasn't going to take the fall for a prank I didn't actually pull off. Even if it was one of the most epic Garrett pranks ever!

CHAPTER 27 - THE BEGINNING OF THE END

Lynn's departure

My wife Lynn was at her wits end. Communications was almost always short of dispatchers due to frequent turnover. The ones who were there were forced to start working twelve-hour shifts six days per week in order to have enough people to cover dispatch, take phone calls for service, train new dispatchers, and work the window if there were citizen walk-in complaints.

It was a stressful job made even more stressful because days off would unexpectedly get cancelled and vacations scheduled and approved well in advance may be cancelled last minute whether the dispatcher had already spent money on a non-refundable vacation deposit or not.

She decided to seek a new career. She was the first Garrett to leave employment with the department. When she turned in her notice, my brother Gary jokingly called her a traitor. It didn't bother her one bit. She was just glad to be out from under the stress.

Eventually, she went to work at a major insurance company that happened to have a large operations center in Winter Haven. She worked her way up to an underwriter position. This new career path made her happy and she had much less stress to deal with. The operations center closed the building at the beginning of the pandemic in 2020. Fortunately, Lynn was able to retain her job and started working from home. At the time of this writing, she's only a few years away from retirement.

My departure

I was so happy as a DARE Officer! I thoroughly enjoyed teaching children and attacking the drug problem from the prevention side of things. My supervisory chain was stellar. Sgt. Kathy Mannet, Lt. Fred Deleon, and Capt. J.J. Staten were absolutely the very best. They didn't micro-manage me and I paid them back by bringing our crime prevention and DARE Unit up to date and constantly generating positive public relations for the department. It had become the best DARE program in the county, dare I say the entire state. But a dark storm was on the near horizon.

There's a saying that goes something like this, "People don't quit jobs, they quit managers." I guess one could say that was what happened to me and the main reason I left law enforcement.

Every so often, there was a department-wide shake-up in personnel. I don't know if this is a strategy the administration learned in some training class for administrators at some point, but in my opinion, it was asinine. If it's not broken, don't fix it. Yet, "fix it" they did.

Supervisors in entire chains of command were redistributed to other departments whether they had any specialized knowledge in the new division or not. Taking a militant SWAT team supervisor and putting him into a supervisory position in a crime prevention role for example just wasn't sympatico. This is very similar to what happened in my case.

The supervisory shake-up came without any warning at all. The most supportive supervisory team I ever had, Sgt. Mannet, Lt. Deleon, and Capt. Staten were all reassigned to other divisions and duties. My new immediate supervisors were Sgt. Jim Butte and Lt. Joel Bent. Butte was a former narcotics officer and SWAT member with a nasty disposition and Bent was an older burned out veteran patrol officer who was rumored to have frequently drank on the job.

Community policing was not their strong point. In fact, it wasn't even on their radars. They were of the philosophy that unless you were on the street, busting heads, and making arrests every day, you weren't a "real" police officer.

Neither of them understood the concept of modern-day law enforcement being like spokes in a wheel like I mentioned earlier in this book. They didn't understand that to combat crime, it needs to be addressed from different angles other than just arresting people. Why two people of this mindset were assigned to the Crime Prevention and DARE Unit is beyond my comprehension.

Friction with Butte and Bent begun almost immediately. Their constant micro-managing and suggestion that Terry and I should answer calls for service in patrol when we weren't teaching caused much of the consternation.

They had no idea how much planning and administrative things we had to do when we weren't teaching, not to mention classroom visitations in all grades other than our regular fifth grade lesson classes. Plus, answering calls for service in patrol meant future days spent in court which would have not only caused scheduling nightmares for us, but for all of the teachers in our schools as well – and teachers operate on VERY tight schedules.

We attempted to explain these concerns to them, but it fell on deaf ears. And we could forget about suggesting any big community projects like our DARE Summer Camp or The Haunted

Crack House because they saw activities such as that as "playing" or "goofing off" and didn't consider it "real police work." Their hardline philosophies prevented them from seeing projects like that as the powerful department public relations tool it was. They were both curt, insulting toward Terry and I, and were just not very nice people to be around. For the first time ever in my law enforcement career, I began to hate coming to work.

Nine months passed and summer was approaching again. Terry and I were in the midst of planning one of our most elaborate DARE graduations ever. Students from all of our schools were to be bussed in and the ceremony was the culmination of the kid's hard work during their seventeen week DARE classes. At the same time, Butte and Bent continued what seemed to be their intentional quest to undo everything Terry and I had built and undermine us every step of the way. I finally had enough.

I came home from work that day frustrated and feeling a lot of anxiety and complained to Lynn – like I had many times before - about the constant hounding and micro-managing which had become a daily occurrence. I spontaneously uttered, "I'm not getting any younger. I should quit the department and start doing magic full time." I was shocked at Lynn's reply. She said, "If you want to perform magic full time, you should do what makes you happy!"

I admit, I was a bit stunned by her response, but she of all people knew how stressful working at the police department could be. Especially when you didn't have a supportive chain of command in place. We talked all night about it. My income from performing magic was almost exactly what I was making per year at the department.

With all of my new free time, I could focus more on promoting myself and increase my performances and the income I made from them. We decided that night that I would resign from the department but only AFTER the big DARE graduation was over. I didn't want to leave before that and disappoint all those kids.

The DARE graduation day came and it was a huge success. The smiles on the kid's faces and excitement in the air about their commitment to stay drug free made me euphoric! I knew I was going to miss the kids when I retired and in the back of my mind, there was a small voice that said, "Maybe you shouldn't resign. Maybe you should just tough it out."

A comment by Butte immediately following the graduation snapped me out of that however. He said to me while the kids were still filing out of the building, "Now that graduation is over, maybe you can start being a real cop."

The following day, I turned in my two-week notice. You know it's funny. Not one person in the department acknowledged my resignation. Not one person in my chain of command asked me why I was leaving or tried to talk me out of it. I wasn't even asked to do an exit interview. It was all a bit surreal.

CHAPTER 28 - THE END BUT THE BEGINNING

When I left the department and started performing magic full time, I met two gentlemen, Bob and Rick, after one of my shows for an outdoor Fourth of July community festival in Haines City, Florida.

They said they were from a movie studio in Orlando. They told me they were directors and we exchanged business cards. They shared with me how much they had enjoyed my show and said, "We'd like to buy you lunch at the studios sometime soon." I replied, "Sure, sounds good."

When we parted ways, Lynn asked me what I thought. With my police officer suspicion radar on high alert, I told her, "They're probably scam artists." She asked, "what about their business card?" I looked at their card again and scoffed. I replied, "I could print something that looks just as legit on our home printer." I put their card back in my pocket and didn't give it or them any more thought.

A few weeks later I got a phone call from Ellen who helped operate their production company. Ellen connected me to Rick and he invited me to their office on the backlot at the movie studio for a lunch meeting with he and Bob. I accepted mainly out of curiosity. But even as I was driving there, I was still thinking, "This is some sort of scam, but I'm going to see how far it goes before they ask me for money."

I pulled up to the guard gate as they had instructed me to, and sure enough, there was a backlot drive-on pass waiting for me. I later learned that drive-on passes at a movie studio back-lot are highly coveted and usually reserved for VIP's only.

I drove up to their office building and noticed five or six parking spaces reserved specifically for their production company. The name of their production company on their business card was actually on the parking space signs. I remember thinking to myself, "OK, if this is a scam, it is one of the most detailed, elaborate scams I have ever seen!"

It wasn't a scam at all. They both raved about my performance they had seen two weeks before. They thought that not only was the magic tricks I performed amazing, but they thoroughly enjoyed my comedy and comical personality.

During our lunch, they pitched me an idea to star in a movie that taught the viewer magic tricks. I told them I was interested but would let them know after I talked it over with my wife. I was actually buying time to call my police buddies and have criminal background checks conducted on them. When you've been a police officer for as long as I had been, you have trust issues.

They checked out ok and after several more meetings over several more months, and signing a financially generous contract with their attorney, I was cast along with a famous and popular comedian/actor to star in the movie.

One of my conditions though, was that I and I alone get to choose which magic tricks were to be revealed. The number one rule in magic is to never reveal how magic tricks are accomplished. I didn't want major magic industry secrets being made available to the general public. The tricks I selected were considered beginner type tricks for people just getting interested in magic. I knew that the material I selected wouldn't upset my brothers and sisters in the magic community.

It was filmed in front of a live audience on the back-lot on one of the studio's largest sound stages. The video was distributed world-wide and is still on the market today. Through Bob and Rick, Lynn and I had the pleasure of meeting a number of Hollywood celebrities. What amazing experiences came about just because of our chance meeting after the show they had seen me perform at that fateful summer day.

Meanwhile, my career and contacts in the magic community started to skyrocket and permitted us to travel to other countries, spend time on cruise ships, and purchase our first home. We had finally obtained a financial independence that eluded us for many years as a law enforcement officer and a dispatcher. But, boy, did I still miss it.

I so dearly loved being a police officer. The opportunities I had to make a difference in some small way in people's lives will always be something I cherish. The adrenaline rushes that occurred at unexpected moments while doing the job was more thrilling than any roller coaster ride you can imagine. The life-long friendships I made with 99% of my fellow officers will be friendships that last the rest of my life. The thousands of children I influenced to follow the right path in life still warms my heart today.

There are times that I wish I were still on the job – even though I'm too old now and not physically able to do it anymore. I will however be a member of the thin blue line fraternity for life. I will be a family member and friend to all of the men and women I served with and to those who are currently serving on the job today.

Although during my career, my call number changed many times at the Sheriff's Office and many times at the Winter Haven Police Department, I will always recall achieving my dream of becoming a law enforcement officer and the pride I felt when I was assigned that very first call number. A number that represents my rewarding, fun, crazy, thrilling, amazing lifetime as a cop. My name will always be 201.

PHOTOGRAPHS

DALE GARRETT AT 10 YEARS OLD WORKING ON PERFECTING HIS CARD FANNING TECHNIQUE. HIS CARD FANS GOT MUCH BETTER IN LATER YEARS.

EARLY PROMOTIONAL PHOTO OF DALE AROUND THE AGE OF THIRTEEN.

ANOTHER EARLY PROMOTIONAL PHOTOGRAPH OF DALE PERFORMING THE CHINESE LINKING RINGS. PHOTO ALSO TAKEN AROUND THE AGE OF THIRTEEN.

DALE AT AGE 19 WORKING THE COMPLAINT DESK IN COMMUNICATIONS AT THE POLK COUNTY SHERIFF'S OFFICE.

DALE ON A FELONY TRAFFIC STOP, PISTOL AT THE READY WHILE WITH THE POLK COUNTY SHERIFF'S OFFICE.

DALE UTTERING HIS TREASURED CALL NUMBER ON THE RADIO – "TWO-OH-ONE TO BARTOW."

DALE WITH THE WINTER HAVEN POLICE DEPARTMENT.

LYNN AND DALE CLOWNING AROUND ON STAGE JUST BEFORE PERFORMING A CORPORATE MAGIC AND COMEDY SHOW.

ABOUT THE AUTHOR

Dale O. Garrett has been an author since 2014. He's a retired police officer and taught the DARE Program to thousands of children in his community during his long career in law enforcement.

He also enjoys spending his time writing comedy scripts for fellow entertainers and helping them with their acts.

Dale created D.O.G. Publishing in May of 2022. D.O.G. Publishing is focused on creating unique content that he hopes will exceed your expectations!

Dale is married. He and his wife Lynn lives with their two Labrador Retrievers in central Florida.

www.ingramcontent.com/pod-product-compliance
Lightning Source LLC
Chambersburg PA
CBHW060523100426
42743CB00009B/1415